PRAISE FOR T

MW00585793

This work flows from the heart of a pastor who knows and practices the art of praying. When you pick up this book from my friend, you will not only learn to pray, but you will learn to pray scripturally in a way that draws you nearer to our loving God.

Patrick N. Poteet
Pastor, Christ Community Church
Frisco, Texas

A wonderful collection of prayers that are both scriptural and thoughtful. I look forward to using many of them in both public worship and my own devotional time.

Mark Bradford
Pastor, St. Stephen's Presbyterian Church
Oklahoma City, Oklahoma

Praying Scripture is among the most profound spiritual experiences the believer can enter into. When a believer uses the very sacred writ itself as a guide to forming his own prayers, he is both listening to God and conversing back with Him at the same time. Both heart and mind are being filled with divine truth and revelation. The lips utter hopeful praises to God, even as God speaks over His people. This is why I am so thankful for Michael Philliber's new collection of prayers. Like *The Valley of Vision*, this collection of Christian confessions, praises, and supplications is thoughtful, reflective, and peaceful. Most of all they are rehearsals of deep Biblical truths. By praying back to God his own Word, we truly "practice" the presence of God. Believers can pray this collection of prayers together or individually. I commend this work highly and am thankful that these prayers were forged in a devoted pastor's study, but framed well for the collective voice of the people of God together in his house on the Lord's Day.

Matthew Everhard
Pastor, Gospel Fellowship PCA
Valencia, Pennsylvania

Michael Philliber's book of prayers help us to put into words the elements of prayer that don't come as easily as our petitions do. His well thought out, Biblical prayers express what is in our hearts but hard to articulate.

Carol Morgan
Midland, Texas

I trust Michael because he loves God's words. I served with him in presbytery for many years, and I always looked forward to his charges to new candidates for ministry because he was so jazzed about the Scriptures and the candidates calling to serve Jesus. I also trust him because when my wife had cancer, I wanted him praying for us, and he was even before he knew we needed it. I will be eternally grateful. These are prayers lifted from the Bible and lived by a man in love with its author, use them to serve the church, your family, and yourself.

David A. Wilson
Director, Bent Tree

If the Holy Spirit helps us in our praying (Romans 8:26), one of the ways he does it is through the teaching and example of faithful pastors. Dr. Michael Philliber's collection of prayers provides us with a fresh vocabulary for our communication with God. The potent prayers in this slender volume express the beauty of pastoral theology as it touches the life of the mind, the broader culture, human suffering, and the world-wide mission of the church. The

Spirit has helped me as I have read and made these prayers my own.
Randy Faulkner
Pastor
Oklahoma City, Oklahoma

My prayers had fallen into a lazy pattern—a simple recipe that sought out God's blessings that were most beneficial to me, sprinkled with a tad of gratitude and a dash of supplication for others. Pastor Philliber's book is a beautiful, useful tool that pushed me deeper into using prayer as an offering of worship, a confession of ignored sin, and a deepening of my relationship with God. Using Scripture as a guide, each prayer connected me to the Word and provided a roadmap to practice the intimacy of prayer with my gracious and loving Father. While this book is not a formula with ten easy steps to a better prayer life, it does provide several models to help the reader lift up their eyes to acknowledge the greatness of God, the state of our broken world, and the call to reach those near and far with the gospel of Christ.
Stacy Schrader
Wife, mom, home-educator, classical tutor

Michael Philliber leaves no stone unturned in this thoughtful and beautiful collection of prayers. This book offers a catholic, holistic, and cathartic aid to Christians of all traditions, not only for its breadth in touching on the ordinary stuff of life, but also for its depth in penetrating the heart of man.
Marq Toombs
Assistant Pastor, Rockwall Presbyterian Church
Rockwall, Texas

You will not read a more engaging book of prayers that gets

to the very essence of our relationship and communication with God.

Anthony B. Holder
Rector, All Saints' Episcopal Church
Jensen Beach, Florida

These prayers can assist those who either don't know how to pray or who otherwise don't feel confident in their ability to pray. For these people, I suggest reading these prayers aloud, perhaps even in small groups. Even those confident in their prayer life may well find examples of new things to pray for, or may find their eyes opened to how better they can pray for others, or pray for specific needs not previously addressed in their own prayer life. Pastors have here yet another tool for forming prayers for use by their congregations, and so too congregations currently without pastors have available to them in this book prayers that may be used as they gather together for worship. Perhaps the greatest benefit of the book is the motivation to take the examples provided and go beyond what is written here, bringing in your own creativity with application to the needs at hand where you are. May our Lord bless his church abundantly as we learn to approach him daily in faith-filled expectation of his mercy and grace.

Wayne Sparkman
Director, PCA Historical Center
St. Louis, Missouri

TO YOU I LIFT UP MY SOUL

CONFESSIONS AND PRAYERS

MICHAEL W. PHILLIBER

ALSO BY WHITE BLACKBIRD BOOKS

Follow whiteblackbirdbooks.pub for upcoming titles and releases.

To the One who wants us to draw near:

אֵלֶ֤יךָ יְהֹוָה֙ נַפְשִׁ֥י אֶשָּֽׂא

ACKNOWLEDGMENTS

I am grateful to Carol Morgan, in Midland, Texas, for encouraging me to pursue this endeavor. It was already on my heart, and her prodding moved me to jump into crafting this book.

Also, for my friend, Doug Serven, who helped me with the typesetting of these pages, and his encouragement.

And for my wife, Anna, who has been in my corner for over forty years and has cheered me on in my recent writing expeditions.

CONTENTS

INTRODUCTION

It is a strange phenomenon. When someone leads public prayer, they either begin to have a truckload of ideas flood their minds and pour out of their mouths that take them across the landscape, from Ziklag to Kadesh. Or, they freeze and can barely get a request to come out, especially a petition that makes any intelligible sense. These have been my own personal experiences as well. Therefore, I felt I had to do something about the situation.

After becoming a pastor, I found that the remedy for my roaming and rambling or stammering and stumbling was to type out most of my public prayers. Whether I am leading a congregation in a corporate confession of sin, or a communal series of prayers, it helps me, and those praying with me, to know that I have a thought-out beginning, middle, and an end. Therefore, over the years, I have scripted and saved a pile of prayers. They have been handy for several settings, and some have been picked up by others for their own personal uses. This little book is a compilation of a number of those prayers.

My purpose in presenting this volume is to give praying people examples and tools that will be an aid in both private and public prayers. It is also for fellow ministers who would like samples of how to lead public prayers. What I have included here is not the only way to pray, and possibly not even the best means, but it is a good approach. I have set them up to cover either 31 days or 31 weeks.

I

REMEMBER NOT MY TRANSGRESSIONS

AUGUSTINE'S CONFESSIONS 1:1, PSALM 37:4, 1:2, 40:8; PROVERBS 1:22, 2:14; PSALM 62:4, 51:3, 1B-2, 10, 12; ROMANS 15:13

To confess and acknowledge our sins and wrongs is a trait my wife and I taught our children, and a practice we seek to habituate ourselves. In more personal settings it is crucial to be specific regarding what we are confessing and about which we are asking forgiveness. It is rarely good enough to simply say, "I'm sorry for everything I ever did that was bad." This often dismisses the offended person's pain and makes light of what we have done. Yet, in public settings confession of sin is more general, simply because of the nature of the event. But a worship leader should allow space for parishioners to silently recollect before the Almighty their specific offenses.

The following prayers for forgiveness have been used in public worship settings for years, some even for decades. But they have also been employed by a few people for their own private devotional times. There are books of common prayer and common worship that have excellent confessions of sin, which I have also used. Yet, I have left those out of this book, and am including only the ones that I have crafted over the years.

If you are planning to utilize any of these in a corporate worship assembly, then the officiant should state what is happening, and give parishioners a moment to soundlessly seek God's mercy for sins that come to mind. After ample time has been given, launch into the confession with a simple pointer-statement, such as, "Now, let us confess our sins together." If you are incorporating these prayers for personal times, then feel free to stop anywhere in the confession to acknowledge specifics that the Holy Spirit brings to your mind.

Lastly, there is no particular order to these thirty-one prayers of confession. At the sensible suggestion of my youngest son, I have presented only thirty-one confessions of sin. This is meant to aid in personal devotions, a different one for each day. I have placed the shaping Scripture reference at the top to give some idea as to the matter contained in each confession. May you find this material helpful, hopeful and wholesome.

1

FOR REFORMATION SUNDAY

PHILIPPIANS 3:2-7

Mighty and merciful Father, reflecting on Paul's biography, it quickly becomes clear that we often forget who you have made us to be and what you have richly given us; and we are confronted by the ways we have put confidence in the flesh. We have been proud of our ethnic heritage, self-reliant because of our nationality, enthralled by our wealth and status, and impressed with our own religious zeal. O God, we confess that we have sought to justify ourselves, by ourselves, to ourselves. And the results have been destructive in our families, our homes, and our lives. Father, all these assurances we now count as loss for the sake of Christ; because you have saved us by grace alone, in Christ alone, to your glory alone, and we receive your loving kindnesses by faith alone. Lord, have mercy. Christ, have mercy. Lord, have mercy. Amen.

SIN, IN SUBTLE AND SIGNIFICANT WAYS

JAMES 3:13-18; DANIEL 9:19

O God, merciful and gracious, longsuffering and abounding in lovingkindness: we have sinned in subtle and significant ways. Our conduct has not always shown the meekness of wisdom. Rather, there have been seasons and times of bitter jealousy and selfish ambition in our hearts, which means we have boasted and been false to the truth. And with this jealousy and selfish ambition have come disorder and every vile practice. Forgive, Father, for Christ's sake. Wash us clean from our sins; and pour into our hearts the wisdom from above that is first pure, then peaceable, gentle, open to reason, full of mercy and good fruits, impartial and sincere. O Lord, hear; O Lord, forgive; O Lord, pay attention and act. In the name of our Lord and Savior Jesus Christ, we pray. Amen.

3

WE HAVE NOT LOVED

1 JOHN 4:7–12

O God, you are love; you have loved us before we ever loved you; and you sent your Son to be the propitiation for our sins and that we might have life in him: we acknowledge that we have sinned against you and our fellow Christians. Despite your rich love toward us, we have not loved you with our whole heart, and we have not loved our brothers and sisters well. We have not often allowed your love for us to guide us in loving one another. With repentant hearts we ask you, and we ask each other: please forgive me. Amen.

SOBER JUDGMENT

ROMANS 5:8-10; 12:3-6; LUKE 18:13-14

O God, you demonstrated your love for us in that while we were sinners, Christ died for us. And while we were your enemies you reconciled us to yourself by the death of your Son and have saved us by his life. We have sinned against you and against one another. We confess that we have not always used sober judgment but have thought more highly of ourselves than we ought. We have not regularly bene-fited one another with the gifts you gave us; or we have exercised those gifts only for ourselves. With the tax collector we bow our heads and beat our breasts, saying: God, be merciful to me, a sinner! Amen.

LET NO INIQUITY GET DOMINION

PSALM 119:33-35, 105, 131-133; ROMANS 8:3-4

Truly, O Lord, your word is a lamp to my feet and a light to my path; but I have not always kept your statutes to the end, nor observed your law with my whole heart, nor delighted in your commandments. Yet you are merciful and gracious, longsuffering and abounding in goodness and truth. Therefore, I open my mouth and pant, because I long for your commandments. Turn to me and be gracious to me, as is your way with those who love your name. Keep steady my steps according to your promise, and let no iniquity get dominion over me. We ask this in the name of your Son, Jesus Christ, in whom you condemned sin in the flesh, in order that the righteous requirement of the law might be fulfilled in us, who walk not according to the flesh but according to the Spirit. Amen.

6

EVIL, UNBELIEVING HEARTS

LUKE 15:21; HEBREWS 3:12–19; MICAH 7:18–19;
REVELATION 1:5

O God, we have sinned against heaven and in your sight, and are not worthy to be called your children. We confess that at times we have bordered on having evil, unbelieving hearts. We confess that we have been known to dabble with deceitful sin. We confess that there have been moments we have hardened our hearts so as not to hear you. Yet you do not retain your anger forever because you delight in mercy. Therefore, have compassion on us, subdue our iniquities, casting all our sins into the depths of the sea; for the sake of him who loves us and freed us from our sins by his own blood, Christ Jesus your Son and our Savior. Amen.

LIGHT WITH DARKNESS

LUKE 15:21; MICAH 7:18–19; 2 CORINTHIANS 6:14,
7:1; REVELATION 1:5

We confess to you, O God, that we have sinned against heaven and in your sight; and are not worthy to be called your children. At times we have attempted to build a partnership between righteousness and lawlessness. At times we have tried to bring into fellowship light with darkness. Yet you do not retain your anger forever because you delight in mercy. Therefore, have compassion on us, subdue our iniquities, casting all our sins into the depths of the sea; for the sake of him who loves us and freed us from our sins by his own blood, Christ Jesus your Son and our Savior. And help us to cleanse ourselves from every defilement of body and spirit and bring holiness to completion in the fear of God. Amen.

8

FUNCTIONED LIKE ATHEISTS

LUKE 15:21; HEBREWS 11:1-3, 6; MICAH 7:18-19;
REVELATION 1:5

We confess to you, O God, that we have sinned against
heaven and in your sight; and are not worthy to be called
your children. We acknowledge that there have been
seasons when assurance of things hoped for has run thin,
and conviction of things not seen has turned into skepti-
cism. We admit that there have been moments when we
have functioned like atheists, responding to life as if you
didn't exist and don't reward those who seek after you. Yet
you do not retain your anger forever because you delight in
mercy. Therefore, have compassion on us, subdue our iniquities, casting all our sins into the depths of the sea; for the
sake of him who loves us and freed us from our sins by his
own blood, Christ Jesus your Son and our Savior. Amen.

SHEEP GONE ASTRAY

ISAIAH 53:6; PSALM 69:5–6; 1 PETER 2:1

We confess to you, O God, that all we like sheep have gone astray; we have turned, everyone, to his own way; and you have laid on Christ the iniquity of us all. O God, you know my foolishness; and my sins are not hidden from you. Let not those who wait for you, O Lord GOD of hosts, be ashamed because of me; let not those who seek you be confounded because of me, O God of Israel. O God cleanse me! And give me the strength to lay aside all malice, all deceit, hypocrisy, envy, and all evil speaking; for Christ's sake. Amen.

10

WASH ME

PSALM 51:1-4, 10, 12; MATTHEW 20:28

Have mercy upon me, O God, according to your lovingkindness; according to the multitude of your tender mercies, blot out my transgressions. Wash me thoroughly from my iniquity and cleanse me from my sin. For I acknowledge my transgressions, and my sin is always before me. Against you, you only, have I sinned, and done this evil in your sight – that you may be found just when you speak, and blameless when you judge. Create in me a clean heart, O God, and renew a steadfast spirit within me. Restore to me the joy of your salvation and uphold me by your generous Spirit; for the sake of your Son, Jesus Christ, who came to give his life a ransom for many. Amen.

MY INIQUITIES HAVE GONE OVER MY HEAD

PSALM 38:1-5, 17-18

O Lord do not rebuke me in your wrath, nor chasten me in your hot displeasure! For your arrows pierce me deeply, and your hand presses me down. There is no soundness in my flesh because of your anger, nor any health in my bones because of my sin. For my iniquities have gone over my head; like a heavy burden they are too heavy for me. My wounds are foul and festering because of my foolishness. For I am ready to fall, and my sorrow is continually before me. For I will declare my iniquity; I will be in anguish over my sin.

12

MY HOPE

PSALM 130:1–4, 39:7–8, 51:12, 15–17

Out of the depths I have cried to you, O Lord; Lord, hear my voice! Let your ears be attentive to the voice of my supplications. If you, Lord, should mark iniquities, O Lord, who could stand? But there is forgiveness with you, that you may be feared. And now, Lord, what do I wait for? My hope is in you. Deliver me from all my transgressions; do not make me the reproach of the foolish. Restore to me the joy of your salvation and uphold me by your generous Spirit. O Lord open my lips, and my mouth shall show forth your praise. For you do not desire sacrifice, or else I would give it; you do not delight in burnt offering. The sacrifices of God are a broken spirit, a broken and a contrite heart—these, O God, you will not despise.

13

HEAL ME

JEREMIAH 17:9-10, 14; PSALM 86:4-5

Truly, O Lord God, my heart is deceitful above all things, and desperately wicked; who can understand it? You, O Lord, search the heart; you test the mind, even to give every man according to his ways, according to the fruit of his doings. Heal me, O Lord, and I shall be healed; save me, and I shall be saved, for you are my praise. Rejoice the soul of your servant, for to you, O Lord, I lift up my soul. For you, Lord, are good, and ready to forgive, and abundant in mercy to all those who call upon you.

14

SIN IS LAWLESSNESS

JAMES 2:10; 1 JOHN 3:4; EZRA 9:6

We acknowledge the truth of your Word, that whoever shall keep the whole law, and yet stumble in one point, he is guilty of all; and that whoever commits sin also commits lawlessness, and sin is lawlessness. Have mercy on us sinners! O our God, we are too ashamed and humiliated to lift up our faces to you, our God; for our iniquities have risen higher than our heads, and our guilt has grown up to the heavens. Now, for Christ's sake, purify us and make us clean. Amen.

LOST SHEEP

LUKE 18:13; PSALM 119:176; 38:4–5; 32:5, 2

O God be merciful to me a sinner! I have gone astray like a lost sheep; seek your servant. For my iniquities have gone over my head; like a heavy burden they are too heavy for me. My wounds are foul and festering because of my foolishness. I acknowledge my sin to you, and I will not hide my iniquity; for truly, blessed is the man to whom you do not impute iniquity. O God be merciful to me a sinner! Amen.

16

IN DISTRESS

LAMENTATIONS 1:20, 3:22-23, PSALM 25:11

See, O Lord, that I am in distress; my soul is troubled; my heart is overturned within me, for I have been very rebellious. For your Name's sake, O Lord, pardon my iniquity, for it is great. Through the Lord's mercies in Christ we are not consumed, because his compassions fail not. They are new every morning; great is your faithfulness, O Lord!

17

NEW EVERY MORNING

LAMENTATIONS 1:20, 3:22–23; 1 PETER 4:7–10;
PSALM 25:11

See, O Lord, that I am in distress; my soul is troubled; my heart is overturned within me, for I have been very rebellious. I have not consistently shown self-control or been sober-minded; I have not dependably loved others with earnestness or happily shown hospitality; and I have not regularly used the gifts you have given me to serve others. For your Name's sake, O Lord, pardon my iniquity, for it is great. Through the Lord's mercies in Christ we are not consumed, because his compassions fail not. They are new every morning; great is your faithfulness, O Lord!

WE DID NOT SERVE YOU

NEHEMIAH 9:32-35

Now, therefore, our God, the great, the mighty, and the awesome God, who keeps covenant and steadfast love, you have been righteous in all that has come upon us, for you have dealt faithfully and we have acted wickedly. We have not kept your law or paid attention to your commandments and your warnings that you gave us. Even in our own country, and amid your great goodness that you gave us, and in the large and rich land that you set before us, we did not serve you or turn from our wicked works. Have mercy on us for Christ's sake, and grant us your peace. Amen.

WE ARE NOT HIDDEN FROM YOUR FACE

JEREMIAH 16:17; PSALM 90:7–8; 130:3–4

O Lord God, your eyes are on all our ways; we are not hidden from your face, nor is our iniquity hidden from your eyes. You have set our iniquities before you, our secret sins in the light of your countenance. If you, Lord, should mark iniquities, O Lord, who could stand? But there is forgiveness with you that you may be feared. In this hope, then, we ask you to forgive us our sins, and cleanse us from all our unrighteousness; for the sake of Christ's death for us. Amen.

20

KEEP BACK YOUR SERVANT

JEREMIAH 16:17; PROVERBS 28:13; PSALM 19:13-14

O Lord God, your eyes are on all our ways; we are not hidden from your face, nor is our iniquity hidden from your eyes. Truly, he who covers his sins will not prosper, but whoever confesses and forsakes them will have mercy. Hear our confession, merciful Father, and forgive us for Christ's sake. Please keep back your servant from presumptuous sins; let them not have dominion over me. Then I shall be blameless, and I shall be innocent of great transgression. Let the words of my mouth and the meditation of my heart be acceptable in your sight, O Lord, my strength and my Redeemer.

21

MISUSED FREEDOM

PSALM 51:1–3; 1 JOHN 1:9; GALATIANS 5:13;
ROMANS 4:25

Have mercy upon me, O God, according to your lovingkindness; according to the multitude of your tender mercies, blot out my transgressions. Wash me thoroughly from my iniquity and cleanse me from my sin. For I acknowledge my transgressions, and my sin is always before me: I concede that I, at times, have used my freedom as an opportunity for the flesh, rather than through love serving brothers and sisters. Forgive us our sins and cleanse us from all our unrighteousness; for the sake of Christ, who gave himself for our offenses and was raised for our justification. Amen.

22

WE HAVE DONE WICKEDLY

DANIEL 9:4-10

O Lord, great and awesome God, who keeps his covenant and mercy with those who love him, and with those who keep his commandments; we have sinned and committed iniquity, we have done wickedly and rebelled, even by departing from your precepts and your judgments. Neither have we heeded your servants the prophets, who spoke in your name. O Lord, righteousness, mercy and forgiveness belongs to you, but to us shame of face, because of the unfaithfulness and rebellion which we have committed against you.

23

OUT OF OUR HEARTS

MATTHEW 15:18-20

O Lord, we acknowledge that your Word is true, and confess that the things which proceed out of our mouth come from our heart, and these have defiled us. For out of our hearts proceed evil thoughts, murder, adultery, sexual immorality, theft, false witness, and slander. These are the things which defile a person. O Lord have mercy on us sinners and forgive our sins for Christ's sake. Amen.

24

UNITE MY HEART

PSALM 103:8–10; 86:11–13

O Lord, you are merciful and gracious, slow to anger, and abounding in mercy. You will not always strive with us, nor will you keep your anger forever. You have not dealt with us according to our sins, nor punished us according to our iniquities. Teach me your way, O Lord; I will walk in your truth; unite my heart to fear your name. I will praise you, O Lord my God, with all my heart, and I will glorify your name forevermore. For great is your mercy toward me, and you have delivered my soul from the depths of Sheol.

25

IF WE DO NOT REPENT

JOEL 2:12-14; LUKE 13:1-5

Merciful and gracious God, slow to anger and abounding in steadfast love: we confess that we have sinned against you in our thoughts, with our words, and by our actions. We have left undone the things we should have done; and we have done the things we should not have done. We have also often thought others were truly worthy of condemnation and catastrophe, while we were more righteous than they, and deserving only peace and plenty. Yet we acknowledge that we have not loved you with our whole heart; we have not loved our neighbors as ourselves; and that if we do not repent, we will likewise perish. We are truly sorry and we return to you with rent hearts. For the sake of your Son Jesus Christ, have mercy on us and forgive us; that we may delight in your will, and walk in your ways, to the glory of your Name. Amen.

26

PERVERSITY OF THE WICKED

AUGUSTINE CONFESSIONS 1:1, PSALM 37:4, 1:2,
40:8; PROVERBS 1:22, 2:14; PSALM 62:4, 51:3, 1B-2,
10, 12; ROMANS 15:13

O Lord, you awaken us to delight in your praise; for you have made us for yourself, and our hearts are restless until they rest in you. But our delight has not been in you; we have not delighted in your law, nor have we found delight in doing your will. Instead, we confess, we have delighted in our own scorning, in the perversity of the wicked, and in lies, blessing with our mouths, but cursing inwardly. O God, we acknowledge our transgressions, and our sin is ever before us! Blot out our transgressions, wash us thoroughly from our iniquity, and cleanse us from our sin. Create in us a clean heart, O God, and renew a steadfast spirit within us. Restore to us the joy of your salvation for the sake of Christ Jesus, that we may be filled with all joy and peace in believing, so that we may abound in hope by the power of the Holy Spirit. Amen.

27

LOVED THE WORLD

EXODUS 34:6; 1 JOHN 2:15–17; 1 JOHN 1:7, 9

Almighty God, who is merciful and gracious, slow to anger, and abounding in steadfast love and faithfulness; we confess that many times we have loved the world and the things in the world, with all of the desires of the flesh, the desires of the eyes and pride of life. We acknowledge that this love is not from you, Father, but is from the world. And we recognize that the world is passing away along with its desires, but whoever does the will of God abides forever. Forgive us for this wayward love; forgive us for pursuing the errant desires of our world. We humbly and repentantly ask your forgiveness because you are faithful and just to forgive us our sins and to cleanse us from all unrighteousness, and because the blood of Jesus your Son cleanses us from all sin. Amen.

SOUGHT OUT OTHER SALVATIONS

1 CORINTHIANS 8:1–6; PSALM 56:9; GALATIANS 2:20

Although there may be so-called gods in heaven and on earth, yet we declare and affirm that there is one God, the Father, from whom are all things and for whom we exist; and one Lord, Jesus Christ, through whom are all things and through whom we exist. Therefore, please forgive us as we have strayed away from you and sought out other salvations; forgive us for looking within, satisfied in our own ability and aptitude; forgive us when we have been puffed up with knowledge; and forgive us for not building up with love. Thank you that you are the God who is for us; and that your Son loved us and gave himself for us. Amen.

29

WEALTH

DEUTERONOMY 8:11–18; EPHESIANS 5:5; 1
TIMOTHY 6:17–19; 1 JOHN 1:7

O Lord our God, you warned us that when we have eaten and are full, built good houses and live in them, have gained plenty of property and been prospered, that we would be enticed to lift our hearts, forget you, and turn from your ways. You warned us that we would be tempted to say in our hearts 'My power and the might of my hand have gotten me this wealth.' But, Lord, it is you who have given us power to get wealth, flourish and prosper. Forgive us for our pride; for covetousness, which is idolatry; for forgetting you by not keeping your commandments and rules and statutes. And since you richly provide us with everything to enjoy, empower us to do good, to be rich in good works, to be generous and ready to share, thus storing up treasure for ourselves as a good foundation for the future, so that we may take hold of that which is truly life. We confess our sins and seek forgiveness because you have promised that the blood of Jesus Christ your Son cleanses us from all sin. Amen.

30

ABUNDANCE AND POSSESSIONS

LUKE 12:15, 16:15

Lord Jesus, you once said, "Take care, and be on your guard against all covetousness, for one's life does not consist in the abundance of his possessions," and you told those who were lovers of money, "God knows your hearts. For what is exalted among men is an abomination in the sight of God." We confess to you our covetousness, and our coddling what is exalted among men. We confess to you that there have been times when we have been stingy and cramped, skimpy and miserly. We who have received such abundant love and grace from you, cry to you to forgive us these sins and all others. Wash us clean and renew our ways and means, for Christ's sake. Amen.

NOT BEING OR DOING WHAT YOU REQUIRE

ADAPTED FROM THE CHILDREN'S FIRST CATECHISM

O Lord God, you have made us and all things, and all for your own glory. We are to glorify you by loving you and doing what you command; and we are to glorify you because you made us and take care of us. But Lord we have sinned: by not being or doing what you require, and by doing what you forbid. And so, now instead of being holy and happy, we have become sinful and miserable; born guilty, sinful and corrupt in every part of our being; and our sin deserves your wrath and curse. Please forgive all my sins, accept me as righteous through Christ, and make me more and more holy in heart and conduct. Amen.

II

GIVE EAR TO MY WORDS,
O LORD

Prayer is a gracious gift opened to us by God. He invites us to pour out our concerns, to cast our burdens on him who cares for us (1 Peter 5:7). Also, the Church, after Pentecost, was known not only for devoting itself to the Apostles' teaching, breaking of bread and fellowship, but it was known for being a praying people (Acts 2:42). Prayer, as communion and communication with God, through Jesus Christ, in the Spirit, is a mark of what it means to be the people of God.

But it is unfortunate when we, privately and publicly, allow our praying to boil down to our own self-concerns and self-preservations. Paul reminded young pastor Timothy that we should be praying for national and international leaders, and geopolitical events, so that all might be saved and God's people might live quiet and peaceful lives (1 Timothy 2:1–4). Based on this injunction, the following prayers are ways I have led my congregations to petition God.

These are congregational prayers, since this is what the gathered people of God engage in and say "Amen" to (1

Corinthians 14:16). In that regard, there are places where there are ellipses, open spaces for the pastor and congregants to mention specific people by name. This fosters attentiveness to the prayers, and participation.

And they are pastoral prayers. They are concerned with pain, fear, disease, health, success, the Kingdom of Christ, churches, nations, and so forth. It has been my custom for many years, to pray for other congregations by name. This includes churches outside my own tradition. I customarily follow the yellow pages in their alphabetical listings of congregations. But for this volume, I have removed those names and the reader will see ellipses where I would naturally mention specific congregations.

Further, these congregational/pastoral prayers have appeared in some form on my blog, *Deus Misereatur*. I have shared my work for years with the intent of helping my parishioners and fellow ministers. There are far more than the ones printed in these pages, which you can find at mphilliber.blogspot.com.

Once more, following the sensible advice of one of my sons, I have limited the number of these prayers to thirty-one. You can use a different one each day. And you can couple it with the confessions of sin in the previous chapter.

Each of these intercessions are either informed by Scripture or shaped by Scripture, in various styles. I find this format helpful and one way of exhibiting our subordination to God's Word as the final rule of faith and life. As the ancient rule of thumb puts it, *lex orandi, lex credenda*: the language of prayer is the language of faith.

1

A NEW YEAR

Almighty God, *though a man's heart plans his ways, it is you who directs his steps* (Proverbs 16:9); therefore, we pray—O director of our steps—for this world and your Church.

Lord God, as we plan our ways for this new year, guide us inch-by-inch and mile-by-mile. May our confidence in you increase throughout the coming days. May we come to know you more than ever before, love you more deeply than we have in the past, and serve you with greater enjoyment and enthusiasm. May we have eyes to see you doing great things—even in the modest and mundane moments. May we have hearts and voices ready to rejoice in your great goodness, even if the wind gets kicked out of us. May we be known as a people who enjoy making much of you!

We ask you to alleviate the suffering, angst and fretfulness of those who are in dire need of your healing or help (...). Please restore them by filling them with your unsurpassable peace to guard their hearts and minds in Christ Jesus and give them rock-hard reasons to have hope in you through all their trials and troubles.

Please look upon our nation, national leadership, and our State Senators, Legislators and Judiciary. Maintain our liberties and guide us all along the path of your truth and righteousness. Protect and preserve our Military members. Also, for the nations of our world and the leaders of the nations, we pray. For the glory of your Name, the good of your Church and wellbeing of all, please reinstate peace, order and sensibility where there is only war and chaos; and build strong justice and hope in the more stable countries.

God, who not only created all things by the word of your power, but cares for creation, and tends it: Please pour out fertility and fruitfulness upon our soil, forests, seas and frontiers that we may enjoy the bounty of your earth, as we join with you in tending and caring for creation.

O Lord, we pray for your Church in all places, for this congregation, and these churches (...). Help us all that we may truly be a people saturated and flourishing in your graciousness, loving our brothers and sisters in Christ, eschewing evil and error in our congregations and out in our communities, and living as your special people zealous for good works.

Finally, we plead for the salvation, transformation and rescue of those who have never believed in your Son and turned from their sins and the restoration of those who have strayed away from you (...). All of these requests we have mentioned, and those that have remained silent on our hearts, we ask in the name of—and by the authority of —Jesus Christ, your Son and our Saving Lord. Amen.

2

HARVEST

Our help is in the name of the LORD, who made heaven and earth
(Psalm 121:2). Hear us, O Lord our help, and for Christ's
sake answer us.

O Lord of the Harvest, have regard to the prayers of
your servants in this church; send us forth as laborers into
your harvest; fit and prepare us by your grace for our vocation and ministry; increase in us the Spirit of power, love
and a sober-mindedness; strengthen us to endure hardships as good soldiers of Jesus Christ; and grant that your
Holy Spirit may prosper our work, so that by our life and
doctrine we may show forth your glory and be instru-
mental in the salvation of many.

Look upon your Church throughout the world,
including these congregations (...). Give your Church your
comforting, courage-inspiring aid. Strengthen your people
in their longing to serve you more faithfully and cause
them to succeed in genuine godliness. And reform what is
awry and askew.

O Lord God, the Almighty, the Most High, we plead
with you to turn your face to look upon the USA. Do not
forsake us nor give us over to what we may deserve, but
instead turn us toward you, and spur us on to chastity,

sobriety, virtuous living, generosity and equanimity. Protect us from all enemies, foreign and domestic, and guide our governmental leaders to remember and retain their vocation, to wit: "to form a more perfect Union, establish Justice, insure domestic Tranquility, provide for the common defense, promote the general Welfare, and secure the Blessings of Liberty to ourselves and our Posterity."[1]

We implore your kindest care and compassion on the nations of our world, especially where there is so much that is violent and vicious (...). We pray that your protection and peacefulness, law and order would overcome all. We also pray that you would restore and refurnish the lives and livelihoods of those who have been trampled upon.

O God Most High, giver of all good gifts, who provides our daily sustenance and wellbeing, we ask you to lift up those who are dispirited in body or mind, who are grieved or terribly troubled with fear and anxiety. We especially ask your care for these (...). Grant them recovery and restored health.

Finally, we call to mind family, friends, neighbors, co-workers, enemies, and acquaintances who have not confessed Jesus Christ as Lord and who continue to walk in darkness; as well as those who have turned away from the Christian Faith (...). Save them, O Lord. All of these requests we have mentioned, and those that have remained silently on our hearts, we ask in the name of Jesus Christ, your Son and our Saving Lord. Amen.

---

1. From the Preamble of the Constitution of the United States.

3

RECONCILED

O our Lord and our God, who has reconciled us to yourself, and to one another, by the death of your Son, having taken away the dividing wall of hostility through his cross (Ephesians 2:14–16), we pray for your World and your Church, and we pray in the name of Jesus who is our peace.

We pray for the wrecked and the robust nations of this world, have mercy. We pray you to safeguard your Church in every land by granting each country a wholesome tranquility, healthful affluence, and honest government.

Almighty God, hear our spoken and unspoken discomforts, worries and fears about the fiscal, political and governmental future of our country. Have mercy on our country, our president, the House and Senate, and bestow and bring about what is best for the good of the populace of this nation and the health of your Church.

Compassionate Father, we remember these who are in need (…). Restore them body and soul, give them peace of mind and joy in the Holy Spirit.

We pray for the people in our lives and on our hearts, who are drifting into perilous places, and those who are thoughtlessly tripping along the path of harmful ways that may well lead them astray (…). Please restrain them and draw them out of danger, deception and defection. Also, for those who have never repented of their sins and trusted in Christ Jesus your Son, especially any who are here now, and those in our families (…). Grant them to call on the name of the Lord and be saved.

We pray for your Church throughout the world, including (…). Guide your people in all places, by your holy Word and Holy Spirit along the way of your truth and righteousness. For those that have stumbled off the mark, may they remember that those you love you rebuke and discipline, and may they become zealous and repent. And take care of all of your peoples' financial, physical and fellowship needs.

For this congregation we implore you: come and strengthen the faithful, arouse any who might be careless, restore the repentant, restrain any who might be reckless, reclaim any who might be wayward, steady the tottering, protect the children, embolden the weak, heal the wounded, encourage the discouraged, calm the worried, give peace to the troubled, comfort to the afflicted, and give joy to us all. And may we be eaters and relishers of your word, for because of Jesus we are called by your name, O Lord, God of hosts (Jeremiah 15:16). Amen.

4

HELP US, LORD

Glory be to God on high: and on earth peace, good will towards men. We praise you, we bless you, we worship you: we glorify you, we give thanks to you for your great glory!

O Great King and Sovereign look upon our country and the nations of this world and move over the plans and intentions of our State Senators and Judiciary. May all come to know your peace on earth, becoming men and women of goodwill.

O God of armies send forth your hosts to preserve and protect our firefighters, police officers, sheriffs, deputies, and troopers, and our military members, particularly those who are close to danger, at home or abroad (...).

Yahweh Rapha, Lord our healer, sustain and direct our doctors, PAs, nurses, First Responders, and specialists—especially those who are on call or working now. Thank you for their help and availability; and may they know they are appreciated.

Lord God whose steadfast love is great above the heavens; whose faithfulness reaches to the clouds (Psalm 108.4), pour out your refreshment and restoratives on those who are parched and paltry (...) that they and we may rejoice in your care and goodness.

O Lord who hears our prayer, who sees our tears, who is the One who heals us (2 Kings 20:5); there are many who are immobilized by tragedy, unbearable conditions, physical and mental anguish, and privations; and there are several who are carrying around deep sadness and grief (...). Please raise them up, delivering and restoring them, hip and thigh, body and soul, inside and out, that they may find good cheer in your Christ and in your kindness, and happily and freely serve you all the rest of their days.

O Lord, who invites all to seek you while you may be found; to call upon you while you are near; who invites the wicked to forsake his way, and the unrighteous man his thoughts; who beckons all to return to you, that you may have compassion on them, and to abundantly pardon them (Isaiah 55.6–7): by your Spirit's enlivening, turn around the hearts and lives of those who have consistently rejected you that they would embrace Christ Jesus freely offered to us in the Gospel.

O our God, our rock, in whom we take refuge, our shield, and the horn of our salvation, our stronghold and our refuge, our Savior who saves us from violence (2 Samuel 22:3); help your Church in this world, including this congregation, as well as (...). As we have come to Jesus, and point all people to Christ, may we remember that he is our peace and has drawn us out of our tribalism, political partisanship and ethnic pride, to become one new man in him.

Hear our Prayer, O Lord; and let our cry come to you, because of your Son, Jesus. Amen.

5

MATTHEW 5:44-46

Ah Holy Father, our Lord Jesus once proclaimed: *"But I say to you, Love your enemies and pray for those who persecute you, so that you may be sons of your Father who is in heaven. For he makes his sun rise on the evil and on the good, and sends rain on the just and on the unjust. For if you love those who love you, what reward do you have? Do not even the tax collectors do the same?"* (Matthew 5:44–46). Therefore, we praise you who sends sun and rain on the just and the unjust, who provides food for the good and the evil, thank you for your tender mercies enjoyed by so many.

O God and Father of our Lord Jesus Christ, whom the whole heavens adore; let the whole earth worship you, all nations obey you, all tongues confess and bless you; and men, women, girls and boys everywhere love you and serve you in peace through Jesus Christ. We ask this especially for families, neighbors, co-workers, and friends we know (...).[1]

Almighty God, we pray for your Church world-over and for churches in our area, especially (...). We pray that their work, toil, patient endurance and rejection of evil would flourish; that they would not abandon their first love; and that where they have fallen into error or compromised with the world that you would straighten them out and build them up (Revelation 2:1–7).

Lord, we beseech you for this congregation, please grant us the grace we need to withstand the temptations and avoid the infections of the world, the flesh and the devil; so that with pure heart, sound mind and holy delight we may follow you, our great God and Savior, Jesus Christ, who is alive and reigns with the Father and the Holy Spirit, ever One God. And beat down Satan under our feet.[2]

We are deeply grateful, O God, for our medical professionals, hospitals and clinics. We give you thanks for the medical advances accomplished even in the last forty years; but most of all, we thank you that many women and men have given themselves to the hard work of caring for people. Encourage the weary; strengthen the fatigued; and cheer the diligent.

Father, we know our nation is not spotless. We confess and acknowledge that the USA is not the kingdom of God nor the Church of Jesus Christ; nevertheless, Father, we love our country. It's a blessing to live here, and for that we thank you. Please build up moral sanity among our people and civic sensibility among our governmental leaders. Where decency and virtue are on the decline, wake us up to the train wreck that will be of our own making and grant us to turn around. And, please confer on our country safety from all enemies foreign and domestic.

Our great God, in whose hands is our life, health and wellbeing: hear our prayers for those who are hungry, homeless, and hopeless; for those who are impoverished or imperiled; for those who are suicidal or dismayed; for those who find their bodies stricken or the homes wrecked; for those being hampered with mental or emotional complications; and especially those battered and broken by natural catastrophe (...). Brighten their days with hope and true happiness; grant them patience under their affliction and a cheerful outcome to their infirmity. All of these requests

we ask through our mediator, Jesus Christ your Son and
our Lord. Amen.

---

1. Adapted from (1979) The Book of Common Prayer, and Administration of the Sacraments, and Other Rites and Ceremonies of the Church, (New York, New York: The Church Hymnary Corporation and Seabury Press), 124.
2. Adapted from (1979) The Book of Common Prayer, and Administration of the Sacraments, and Other Rites and Ceremonies of the Church, (New York, New York: The Church Hymnary Corporation and Seabury Press), 214.

6

MATTHEW 6:19–34

"Do not lay up for yourselves treasures on earth, where moth and rust destroy and where thieves break in and steal, but lay up for yourselves treasures in heaven, where neither moth nor rust destroys and where thieves do not break in and steal. For where your treasure is, there your heart will be also." We pray, Lord, for your Church here and world over, including (...). Instead of our looking for earthly fame or fortune, or earthly treasures, replenish her with your own steadying strength, stabilizing aid, resilient love, long-lasting commitment, unwavering godliness and sound doctrine, so that her treasure and heart will always be deposited with you. Through the prayers and work of your Church may your own open-handed help and guidance be shown to all so that sojourners and wayfarers may find shelter; that those blown about by the violence and predation of our vicious world may find sanctuary; that the lonely and deserted may find warmth; and that the broken, bruised and battered may find respite.

"No one can serve two masters, for either he will hate the one and love the other, or he will be devoted to the one and despise the other. You cannot serve God and money." We pray for heretics and hucksters, for those who have never embraced your

Son Jesus Christ, along with those who have once made a good confession and since then made shipwreck of their faith (...). Shine the light of your mercy and grace into their hearts and heads, that they may no longer try to serve two masters, or the wrong master, and bring them to new life in Christ and single-hearted loyalty to you.

"Therefore do not be anxious, saying, 'What shall we eat?' or 'What shall we drink?' or 'What shall we wear?' For the Gentiles seek after all these things, and your heavenly Father knows that you need them all." High King of Heaven, who is never caught unawares, even though the actions of humankind may grieve you; we sincerely implore you to grant our country safety from all enemies foreign and domestic, and cause the people of this nation to know that you are not a tight-fisted God, but an open-handed Father. We also ask you to pour out your merciful kindness on all nations that order, stability, and tranquility may be established for the good of all people, and for the good of your Church.

"But seek first the kingdom of God and his righteousness, and all these things will be added to you. Therefore do not be anxious about tomorrow, for tomorrow will be anxious for itself. Sufficient for the day is its own trouble." O God, heavenly Father, by your Son Jesus Christ you have promised to all those who seek your kingdom and your righteousness that you would care for their necessities; look on those who are straining under the weight of disease, ailments, poverty, penury, depression, mental or physical afflictions, and striving to keep their heads above water; (...). Raise them up from their misery or misfortune, granting them strength and hope that they may be relieved from anxiety, and spend the rest of their lives serving, glorifying and enjoying you: now, always and forever. In Christ's name we pray. Amen.

7

PSALM 23

"The LORD is my shepherd; I shall not want." O God, our hearts are full of thankfulness because we have been richly endowed with your goodness: health, strength, hope, stamina, happiness, sustenance, homes and satisfaction. And even when in your good providence these are withheld from us, we have you, our greatest good and deepest joy! Thank you! Truly, the Lord is my shepherd; I shall not want!

"He makes me lie down in green pastures. He leads me beside still waters. He restores my soul. He leads me in paths of right-eousness for his name's sake." Give strength, aid, increasing love, durable commitment and unwavering godliness to fill and replenish your Church here, as well as (…) and your Church throughout the world. O great Shepherd of your people, where there are wolves in sheep's clothing in your flock, expose and remove them that your people may be restored. Bring your people refreshment and rest in a chaotic world raging with tumults and terrors. With you before us, may we walk happily along the paths of right-eousness for your name's sake.

"Even though I walk through the valley of the shadow of death,

I will fear no evil, for you are with me; your rod and your staff, they comfort me." Our comforting Shepherd, who is not restricted or restrained by our diseases, ailments, or mental and emotional afflictions; we ask you to be with these (…). Raise them from their misery and misfortune, granting them unlooked for strength, hope and comfort that they may fear no evil and may spend the rest of their lives serving, glorifying and enjoying you.

"You prepare a table before me in the presence of my enemies; you anoint my head with oil; my cup overflows." As our nation goes through more and more changes; as what once were unquestionable morals get thrown onto the table to be questioned, slaughtered and mocked; as homes shatter; as lives crumble under various addictions; make your truth shine out more brightly so that our leaders, fellow citizens and fellow residents may see the brilliant correctness and goodness of your ways, and submit happily to your course. For our Soldiers, Sailors, Airmen, Marines, Law Enforcers, Sheriffs, Deputies, Special Agents, and Marshalls, we ask you to protect them as they pass through harm's way; give them strength to exercise honor and integrity, hope in the darkest and bleakest moments.

"Surely goodness and mercy shall follow me all the days of my life, and I shall dwell in the house of the LORD forever." O rescuing Shepherd, there are people who do not know your goodness and mercy, people we love or are acquainted with who have never embraced your Son Jesus Christ, trusting in him for their salvation and repenting of their sin. And there are those we love or are acquainted with who seem to have become hardened by the deceitfulness of sin (…). There are whole tribes, gangs, and countries; there are Iraqis, Afghanis, Nigerians, Somalis, Hans, Yamato peoples, Koreans, Tibetans, Kazakhs, and a host of others that have never heard nor responded to the Gospel of Jesus. We pray for your Gospel to go forth in the power of

the Spirit, to have open access and run swiftly, that those appointed to eternal life may believe (Acts 13:48). We ask these because you are our great shepherd, our good shepherd. Amen.

8

PSALM 111

"Praise the LORD! I will give thanks to the LORD with my whole heart, in the company of the upright, in the congregation. Great are the works of the LORD, studied by all who delight in them." Almighty God, we pray for your Church worldwide, including (...), as well as this congregation. Grant grace to be courageously committed to you; supply all that is lacking, whether valor, assets, good leaders, laborers or open doors. For the shepherds of your Church, help us to maintain true doctrine and the Gospel of Jesus Christ, and may we be truly holy, all for the good of your Church and your glory. And for those in the ministry who are atheists, agnostics, predators, pedophiles, or wolves in sheep's clothing, convert them, and where necessary, remove them and prosecute them.

"Full of splendor and majesty is his work, and his righteousness endures forever. He has caused his wondrous works to be remembered; the LORD is gracious and merciful. He provides food for those who fear him; he remembers his covenant forever." Father, who by your almighty and everywhere present power, upholds—as it were by your hand—heaven, earth, and all creatures, and so governs them that herbs and grass, rain and drought, fruitful and barren years, food and drink,

health and sickness, riches and poverty, come not by chance but by your fatherly hand: In grateful solace and solicitous gratitude, may we be patient when things go against us, thankful when things go well, and for the future have good confidence in you, our faithful God and Father, that nothing in creation will separate us from your love; for we are convinced that all creatures are so completely in your hand that without your will they can neither move nor be moved.[1]

"He has shown his people the power of his works, in giving them the inheritance of the nations. The works of his hands are faithful and just; all his precepts are trustworthy; they are established forever and ever, to be performed with faithfulness and uprightness." We ask you to strengthen those who are fighting against the carnage, inhumanity and evil in their lands. Please stop human trafficking; please stop the harassment of your Church. May all nations come to bow the knee to the Lord Jesus, and goodwill and wellbeing abound in all places. Also, we cry out to you to have mercy on our nation! Change the direction of the people and the rulers that we may become a nation of hard-working, fair-minded, well-educated, morally-sound people; and a hope-giving example to all the countries in our world. Restrain our leaders that they would keep their noses out of places they ought not to be sticking them. And give your aid and strength to all those in the US Armed Forces (…). May they serve devotedly, fearlessly, admirably and honorably.

"He sent redemption to his people; he has commanded his covenant forever. Holy and awesome is his name! The fear of the LORD is the beginning of wisdom; all those who practice it have a good understanding. His praise endures forever!" O Father of mercies and God of all comfort, our only help in time of need: please behold, visit and relieve these (…). Mercifully look upon them; comfort them with a sense of your good-ness; preserve them from the temptations of the enemy; and give them patience under their affliction. In your good

time, restore them to health, and enable them to lead the residue of their life in your fear and to your glory; and grant that finally they may dwell with you in life everlasting. Finally, show your kindness and deploy your saving love to these who have never turned to Christ (...). Amen.

---

1. Heidelberg Catechism 27–28.

9

THE LORD'S PRAYER

"O LORD, I am your servant; I am your servant, the son of your maidservant. You have loosed my bonds. I will offer to you the sacrifice of thanksgiving and call on the name of the LORD. I will pay my vows to the LORD in the presence of all his people, in the courts of the house of the LORD, ... Praise the LORD!" (Psalm 116:16–17, 19c).O Lord, we thank you for saving us from many dangers and devastations, known and unknown; for providing us with livelihoods and loves; for filling us with good things and being a God of steadfast love and faithfulness. Glory to you, O God Most High!

Our Father who art in heaven, hallowed be thy name: O God, how we long to see you honored by all; to be reverenced and held in high regard by presidents and presidential candidates of all parties, constituents and denizens in all regions, by multiple Medias world over, family members, fellow workers, friends and foes. Since the fear of the Lord is Zion's treasure (Isaiah 33:6c), may the hallowing of your name become a premier priority amongst your people. Give your fatherly discipline, deliverance and direction to your Church world over, here in America, this congregation, as well as (...).

Thy kingdom come, thy will be done, on earth as in

heaven: We desire to see your reign filled in and filled out from *"the four winds, from one end of heaven to the other"* (Matthew 24:31). Therefore we intercede on behalf of these missionaries (...) and campus ministers (...); that you would provide support, strength, stamina and success in their work. And be with those who frequent our church playground and our ESL classes, that they would be drawn in to hear the Gospel. And may your kingdom, your reign, come on our country and all nations of this earth.

Give us this day our daily bread: Father, you supply our every need. There are some here who have serious needs (...). Provide them what they have need of. And we confess that all we have, in all of the plenty, comes from you. Help us to be rich in good works, to give abundantly, and to not neglect to do good and to share what we have, for such sacrifices are pleasing to you (Hebrews 13:16).

And forgive us our debts as we forgive our debtors: Instead of holding grudges and demanding our pound of flesh, may your gracious mercy strike us with such weight and force afresh that we would become quick to forgive those who have wronged us, and just as quick to ask forgiveness of those whom we have wronged.

And lead us not into temptation, but deliver us from evil and the evil one: Look mercifully, O Good Shepherd, on this your flock; and suffer not the sheep which you have redeemed with your precious blood to be torn in pieces by the assaults of the devil, the flesh and the world. Thank you that you have rescued us from the penalty of sin, the power of sin, and the pride of sin. We long with earnest yearning for you to return where we will be forever free from the presence of sin!

For thine is the kingdom, and power, and the glory forever. Amen!

10

PSALM 113

Praise the LORD! Praise, O servants of the LORD, praise the name of the LORD! We lift our hearts to you, O mighty God, merciful God, majestic God, because you have cared for us in spiritual and bodily and psychological needs; and so, with our hearts and hands and voices we resound with your praises!!!!

Blessed be the name of the LORD from this time forth and forevermore! From the rising of the sun to its setting, the name of the LORD is to be praised! Lord God, our Father, we pray for your one, holy, catholic and apostolic Church, and we pray for (...). We pray for all your Church's bishops, elders, pastors, ministers, and servers, that they would all be faithful to the Word of God and guide your Church to prove herself to be the light of Christ to the nations. And Abba, Father, for this congregation we pray; for all of our parents and the children in our homes, our students and young adults seeking to take out on their own paths, for each of us in our vocations and conditions; that in all we do we would show ourselves Christ's disciples in word and deed.

The LORD is high above all nations, and his glory above the heavens! Who is like the LORD our God, who is seated on high, who looks far down on the heavens and the earth? Governor and Ruler of all creation, nations and peoples, we pray for the peace and security of the world's nations, for an end to unjust war and violent oppression that the peoples of the earth may come to receive the Prince of Peace. And eternal God, who has made us pilgrims and sojourners, we pray for our own country, for those who govern, for all the people in this land. May we have justice, security and well-being. In these days of racial tensions, political rodeos, hot headedness, terror threats, ethical fluidity, and sexual bewilderment, show yourself a mighty God on our behalf that our own nation would finally say with deep conviction and deliberate comportment, "In God we trust!" We pray for (…) that you would visit him with your mercy and justice: that he would come to his senses and see the evil he ripped through peoples' lives with and he would utterly turn to you; but also that he may receive for his crimes what is legitimately warranted. Finally, for others in our country who are tempted to unjustly take up arms and destroy other—whether out of bigotry, hatred, fear or from mental illness—stop them, in whatever ways are best and right for them.

He raises the poor from the dust and lifts the needy from the ash heap, to make them sit with princes, with the princes of his people. He gives the barren woman a home, making her the joyous mother of children. Praise the LORD! Father, giver of all good gifts, we pray for the poor and hungry (…), the homeless and mentally ill (…), the unemployed and heavily employed (…), the sad and scared (…), the sick and lonely (…), and for the families of the dead and the wounded in these cities (…); that help unlooked for may arrive at just the right time; that you would draw them up from the pit of destruction, out of the miry bog, and set their feet upon a rock, making their steps secure. That you would put a new song in their mouth, a song of praise to our God, so that many will see and fear, and put their trust in the Lord (Psalm

40:2–3). And saving God, we pray for those who do not rest on your Son Jesus—maybe some in here and those out there (...); as well as those who are in deep spiritual need (...); that by your Spirit active in their lives, they may find conviction, courage, and comfort in Jesus Christ. Amen.

11

PSALM 11

In the LORD I take refuge; how can you say to my soul, "Flee like a bird to your mountain, for behold, the wicked bend the bow; they have fitted their arrow to the string to shoot in the dark at the upright in heart; if the foundations are destroyed, what can the righteous do?" O Lord our refuge, the shelter in the midst of the storm, for those who are taunted and teased by their afflictions, ailments, burdens or biliousness to *"flee like a bird to your mountain,"* we pray (…), enfold them in your compassion and fill them with courage that they may rejoice in your goodness. For those being aimed at by the bow of the wicked, shot at in the dark and dimness, we pray (…), shield them from the fiery darts, and screen them from slander and spite. For those who are rocking and reeling and feeling as if the bottom is falling out, we pray (…), may they find in you their sure foundation and be built up in sturdy strength.

The LORD is in his holy temple; the LORD's throne is in heaven; his eyes see, his eyelids test the children of man. The LORD tests the righteous, but his soul hates the wicked and the one who loves violence. O Lord, high and lifted up, many in academia and in positions of power and prominence in our broadcasting and print outlets act and function as if they are gods, high and mighty in their own opinions and derisiveness. Many in our institutions of science and medicine proceed and pronounce as if the sun rises and sets at their bidding. Bring them to know that they are mere dust before you, and that they are faulty and frail mortals who are given each breath and each opportunity to think and speak and live from your hand. And bring them to bow the knee before your Son, Jesus Christ, now, before he returns to judge the living and the dead. And for our own country and all the nations of the world, we pray: *"Arise, O LORD! Let not man prevail; let the nations be judged before you! Put them in fear, O LORD! Let the nations know that they are but men"* (Psalm 9:19–20)!

Let him rain coals on the wicked; fire and sulfur and a scorching wind shall be the portion of their cup. For the LORD is righteous; he loves righteous deeds; the upright shall behold his face. O Father, we pray for your Church that spans this round globe, including this congregation, and (...). You who are righteous and love righteous deeds, may your righteousness triumph among us. Produce repentance where there has been a history of hardheaded recalcitrance; grace where there has been hard-nosed legalism; peace where there have been heartless divisions; hope where there has been helpless trouble; ongoing fortitude where there has been Biblical faithfulness; and outright success where there has been Gospel outreach. Hasten the day when the upright will behold your face; by the saving power of Jesus Christ our Lord. Amen.

12

PSALM 119:161–168

Princes persecute me without cause, but my heart stands in awe of your words. There are places in our world, O Lord, where injustice, immorality, illegality and inhumaneness sit enthroned and empowered, violently and viciously crushing people and seeking to harm your chosen ones. Lift up the downtrodden and demoralized, show strength with your arm; scatter the proud in the thoughts of their hearts; and bring down the mighty from their thrones (Luke 1:51–52). We especially ask for you to defend, direct, and deliver your Church in all places, and more pointedly, where Christians are persecuted today.

I rejoice at your word like one who finds great spoil. Eternal God look upon these United States of America that there may again be great joy at your Word, like the joy of those who have found a priceless treasure. Many who are in office claim to be disciples of Jesus, and fellow believers. Especially for them we beg you to shape their desires, direct their actions, protect their families, and build them up to pursue God-defined justice, equity, and the common good for all in this land—the free born, foreign born and unborn.

I hate and abhor falsehood, but I love your law. Seven times a day I praise you for your righteous rules. Great God, faithful God, God of truth and fidelity; we implore you to bring honesty and integrity to the forefront of our land, to the forefront of our relationships, our families, our jobs, our schools and colleges, our civil offices, and our international affairs. Rouse your people in this country, to include these churches, (…), to reclaim and be reclaimed by the importance of your Word, to return to committed, prayer-full connection with you through Christ alone received by faith alone, and resilience in pursuing what is right.

Great peace have those who love your law; nothing can make them stumble. We have loved ones and friends, O Father, who once professed faith in Christ but now seem to be tottering between heaven and hell, perdition and redemption (…). May they come to the peace your law promotes, the peace that can be found only in your Son, Jesus Christ, and only by the fullness of your Spirit, so that they may become steady and not stumble.

I hope for your salvation, O LORD, and I do your commandments. My soul keeps your testimonies; I love them exceedingly. I keep your precepts and testimonies, for all my ways are before you. Hear us cry out for those who have never known your great salvation: family, friends, neighbors, and any of the kids and parents we interacted with in VBS (…). Bring them into your family that they may know they're forgiven in Jesus Christ, and bear the fruit of the Spirit: love, joy, peace, longsuffering, gentleness, goodness, faith, meekness and self-control. And please grant recovery, refreshment, and restoration for those in tight places, difficult spaces, and hard races (…). Through our great High Priest, Jesus the Son of God, we offer these prayers. Amen.

13

PSALM 87

On the holy mount stands the city he founded; the LORD loves the gates of Zion more than all the dwelling places of Jacob. Glorious things of you are spoken, O city of God. Selah. Sometimes, Lord, we forget that you love the gates of Zion more than all the dwelling places of Jacob. Sometimes we think you should cherish our country more than you do your Church. Sometimes our constitutional concerns become more important to us than the cares of your kingdom. So, remembering that you love the gates of Zion more than all the dwelling places of Jacob, we still pray for our country as you have bidden us to do. Tensions abound on the right hand and on the left. Violence raises its beastly head in brutal and bloody ways. The rhetoric of some seems to pour more petrol on the smoldering embers threatening to ignite into a bursting flame. There are places and spaces of injustice in our courts, on our streets, behind closed doors, and out in open spaces. Therefore, we implore your kindness and goodness to come and smother the seething cinders and to promote fair-mindedness, helpfulness and benevolence. Thank you for the many who are working to foster civility and sanity; those in office, those who patrol neighborhoods and streets, and those who influence their communities.

And we pray for countries that have been bloodied by bandits or are governed by gangsters. Please give relief, justice and restoration.

Among those who know me I mention Rahab and Babylon; behold, Philistia and Tyre, with Cush— "This one was born there," they say. And of Zion it shall be said, "This one and that one were born in her"; for the Most High himself will establish her. The LORD records as he registers the peoples, "This one was born there." Selah. We pray for your Church that meets here, your Church all over the world; for our denomination; and for (...). Where she is facing hard ways in hard places, grant her help and relief. Where she is impoverished and penurious fill her up with all she needs. In the places where she has compromised under the prevailing pressures, bring her to hearty repentance. May her numbers increase, her faith flourish, and her hope be rock solid. We pray that for many from *"Rahab, Babylon, Philistia, Tyre with Cush"* you will register and record, *"This one was born there."* May wayward children be restored to the fellowship of Christ's people and may many, many more who have never believed come to faith in Christ and be numbered among the citizens of Zion from every tribe, tongue, skin color and nation (...). May our VBS and ESL classes be a valuable part of this happening!

Singers and dancers alike say, "All my springs are in you." O Father, as you well know, some find themselves experiencing serious troubles—health, finances, future, family, recovery from surgeries, physical weakness, mental or emotional struggles, and other areas. We ask you on their behalf to raise them up, give them hope, show them better times and better days, and may they feel all the way down into their bones that you will never leave them nor forsake them so that with the singers and dancers they may say, *"All my springs are in you!"* Through Christ our Lord we pray. Amen.

14

PSALM 36

Transgression speaks to the wicked deep in his heart; there is no fear of God before his eyes. For he flatters himself in his own eyes that his iniquity cannot be found out and hated. The words of his mouth are trouble and deceit; he has ceased to act wisely and do good. He plots trouble while on his bed; he sets himself in a way that is not good; he does not reject evil. Our hearts, O God, grieve for those who have never repented of their sins, believed in Christ and avowed him as Lord (...). Save them, work mightily penetrating their resistance and draw them into your family. But we also pray for those whose words are trouble and deceit, who plot trouble on their beds, who set themselves in a way that is not good and don't reject evil: Terrorists, guerrillas, Antifa, Proud Boys, and the KKK; thuggish leaders of nations and blood-spattered rebels; thieves, molesters, muggers, and the high-society promotors of death. O God, restrain and vanquish their bloodlust and bring order and honor to fill the void.

Your steadfast love, O LORD, extends to the heavens, your faithfulness to the clouds. Your righteousness is like the mountains of God; your judgments are like the great deep; man and beast you save, O LORD. Stand up, O God, be present now with your Church gathered here, with your Church world over, with our denomination, and with (...). Protect her from persecutors and pursuers. Fill her with resilient strength to be faithful and firm in her witness of your Son, Jesus Christ. Bring your Spirit of Truth to guide her into all truth, and to turn her away from syncretism with, and surrender to, the pressures of godlessness and greed, materialism and mania.

How precious is your steadfast love, O God! The children of mankind take refuge in the shadow of your wings. They feast on the abundance of your house, and you give them drink from the river of your delights. For with you is the fountain of life; in your light do we see light. We have feasted on the abundance of your house and have drunk from the river of your delights, for you are our fountain of life and in your light we see light. May this church be a vital and valid channel through which your Gospel and good will would go forth into all cities far and wide. Shower your goodness on our programs we do for your glory as well as the churches who partner with us.

Oh, continue your steadfast love to those who know you, and your righteousness to the upright of heart! Let not the foot of arrogance come upon me, nor the hand of the wicked drive me away. There the evildoers lie fallen; they are thrust down, unable to rise. Continue your steadfast love for those burdened by bleakness (...), loaded with lament (...), fraught with fear (...), encumbered with illness. And for the spirit of anger, anxiety, apprehension and aggression that seems to be wafting over our land—save us from it! Cause to blow in a fresh social mindset and outlook that will foster charity and cooperation. Lord, have mercy on us; Christ, have mercy on us; Lord, have mercy on us; and give us your peace! Amen.

15

PSALM 93

The LORD reigns; he is robed in majesty; the LORD is robed; he has put on strength as his belt. Yes, the world is established; it shall never be moved. Your throne is established from of old; you are from everlasting. Since righteousness exalts a nation, but sin is a reproach to any people, we earnestly and heartily pray to you, O reigning God, for our country. Reflecting on the 5th through 10th Commandment, we pray that we and our fellow residents will honor fathers and mothers and all legitimate authorities, instead of affronting aging parents, teachers, police officers or magistrates. We pray that we and the people of this country would turn away from murder in its various shapes and sophistications and would pursue all lawful endeavors to preserve life. We pray that we and the occupants of this land would renounce proud sexual immorality and embrace chastity and life-long monogamy. We pray that we and the inhabitants of our nation would cast aside all ways and means that unjustly hinder our own or our neighbor's wealth and outward estate and would rather engage in legitimate practices of advancing one another's lawful prosperity. We pray that we and the folks within our boarders would discard false witness bearing and would become a people who promote truth and one another's good name. We pray that all would stop hungering and hankering after neighbors' wives, husbands, property and prosperity, and all would grow in charitableness and full contentment with our condition.

"*The floods have lifted up, O LORD, the floods have lifted up their voice; the floods lift up their roaring. Mightier than the thunders of many waters, mightier than the waves of the sea, the LORD on high is mighty!*" We implore you who are enthroned in the heavens, to exercise your special providence toward your Church in this place, at (...); and throughout the world. May civil righteousness and goodness prevail in all lands so that your Church may lead a peaceful and quiet life, godly and dignified in every way; so that the Gospel may speed ahead and be honored, as has happened before.

"*Your decrees are very trustworthy; holiness befits your house, O LORD, forevermore.*" We are very grateful for our country, and the liberties you have bequeathed to us. We are thankful for the various salutary advantages you have entrusted to us. And most of all, we are deeply appreciative of the gifts of your Son and your Spirit in whom we have new life, new standing, and new hope. We pray for friends and family who have never repented of their sins and believed in Christ; and we entreat your restoring, reviving mercies for those who once claimed to be Christians but now are no longer walking with your Son (...). Finally, we beseech your continued provision for this congregation as we look for suitable sisters to take up leadership roles in our women's ministries and as we move closer to VBS. And Lord, we ask for your strength, comfort, mending, and support for those who are sick, ailing, dark, dreary, unsettled, uncertain, grieving or groaning (...). All we ask in Jesus name. Amen.

16

PSALM 131

*O LORD, my heart is not lifted up; my eyes are not raised too high;
I do not occupy myself with things too great and too marvelous for
me.* O Mighty God, high and exalted, you are the greatest
good, you are the utmost in integrity, and you are supreme
over life and death: we acknowledge that humility is a
waning virtue; thinking more highly of ourselves than we
ought, we think ourselves mighty, magnificent and
marvelous in our modern technologies, scientific advance-
ments, social sensibilities, medical feats, and military
competencies. All of this egoism surfaces in our national
and international politics, foreign. policies, and business
ventures. Help us, in our communities and in our country
to remember that we are but human, and therefore *"surely
all mankind is a mere breath"* (Psalm 39:5, 11)! That *"not from
the east or from the west and not from the wilderness comes lifting
up, but it is God who executes judgment, putting down one and
lifting up another"* (Psalm 75:6–7). O Mighty God, high and
exalted; bring us to remember this!

*But I have calmed and quieted my soul, like a weaned child with
its mother; like a weaned child is my soul within me.* Merciful
Father, for those tumbling and tossing about in anxious-
ness and alarm, we pray; for those worn out and worn thin

from sickness, sadness, sorrow or scarceness, we pray; for those who found waking up this morning a challenge, we pray; for those pondering their future and all they can see are storms or privations, we pray; (...). May your presence and peace fill them with quietness and calm, lifting their hearts in hope and wholeness, we pray!

O Israel, hope in the LORD from this time forth and forevermore. O High King of Heaven give your strength and direction to your One, Holy, Catholic and Apostolic Church throughout the world, in this place, and also at (...); as well as for our upcoming General Assembly. Remove all that fosters schism and everything that spawns heresy. Overcome all that breeds racism and bigotry. Restore to us the joy of your salvation and guide us by your Spirit of Truth into all truth. Help us to bear true faith and allegiance to Christ the Lord that with full courage now as always Christ may be honored in our bodies, whether by life or by death. *"For me to live is Christ and to die is gain"* (Philippians 1:20–21).

Thank you for our mission trip to (...). May the people who went, and those we interacted with, be filled with your life, love and liberty in Christ. And for our upcoming VBS we pray that not only will our kids gain richly, but that the others that come will know Jesus Christ the Lord. And please draw in kids and families who are no longer walking with you, or those who have never known you, and may this enterprise bring them to believe in Christ and become his followers all their days! In Jesus name, and for his honor, we pray. Amen.

17

PSALM 127

Unless the LORD builds the house, those who build it labor in vain. Unless the LORD watches over the city, the watchman stays awake in vain. It is in vain that you rise up early and go late to rest, eating the bread of anxious toil; for he gives to his beloved sleep. Lord, you are the One who builds the house, and watches over the city. We plant and water, but you are the one who gives the growth! Bless our congregation with fitting and fair growth; that we would grow roots downward and bear fruit upward; that you would add to our number such as are being saved. And, Mighty God, we pray for your Church all around this marvelous globe, as well as (…); and we pray for our General Assembly. Preserve and protect your Church from scandal and suffering; repair her breaches and breaks with the healing glue of the Holy Spirit; with the supremacy of the Gospel; and with all that accords with sound doctrine. And, Lord, since we are so dependent on you for life, health, wholeness and livelihood, we pray for those who are feeling the slowing effects of age (…); the wearisomeness of having more month than money (…); the cruddy results of sickness, disease, cancer and confusion (…); give to your beloved sleep, rest, fullness, and restoration that they may rise up and sing your praises.

Behold, children are a heritage from the LORD, the fruit of the womb a reward. Like arrows in the hand of a warrior are the children of one's youth. Blessed is the man who fills his quiver with them! He shall not be put to shame when he speaks with his enemies in the gate. High King of Heaven, take care of our country. Prosper, replenish and promote what is good, just, decent, and fair. Bring a change of heart and a change of mind to that which is cramped, crooked, or corrupt. Make America great again, great in ways that are ethical, sensible, and moral. Lead our leaders to truly be *for* America, and *for* the honorable ideals America once stood for. Finally, good Father, we give you thanks for the fathers in our lives, especially those who tried to be good fathers, who toiled to provide and parent well. For the fathers here we ask you to guide and steer them as reflections of your Fatherhood. For those who are heartbroken because of their children's choices and directions, help them to know that you know what that's like so that they would find comfort in being close to you, a Father of many ornery and obstinate children. For those who had absentee, abusive or over-assertive fathers, may there be repentance, reconciliation, and forgiveness before it's too late. In Christ's name, Amen.

18

PSALM 2

Why do the nations rage and the peoples plot in vain? The kings of the earth set themselves, and the rulers take counsel together, against the LORD and against his Anointed, saying, "Let us burst their bonds apart and cast away their cords from us." O God see how the peoples and nations of this world conspire and rage against your Son and his Lordship: through adjudication, legislation, execution of orders, shaming on the air waves, taunting and demonizing through social media and music, and in some places by downright brutality and cruelty. See, O Lord! Take note and come to the aid of your chosen ones. We long to see our own nation flourish as a just and lawful land. We long to see our neighborhoods, cities and State to show themselves to be the land of the free and the home of the brave.

He who sits in the heavens laughs; the Lord holds them in derision. Then he will speak to them in his wrath, and terrify them in his fury, saying, "As for me, I have set my King on Zion, my holy hill." Though all the world scoffs and scorns the coronation of your Son, we and all of your Church, declare him to be Lord, and head of all things to his Church. We pray on behalf of your Church in this place, worldwide, as well as (...). Not only may we bow the knee to your Son, but may we be a people of utmost loyalty to him in our worship and ways, in our liturgy and life. May we not be frightened in anything by our opponents but always live in a manner worthy of the Gospel of Christ.

I will tell of the decree: The LORD said to me, "You are my Son; today I have begotten you. Ask of me, and I will make the nations your heritage, and the ends of the earth your possession. You shall break them with a rod of iron and dash them in pieces like a potter's vessel." For all national and international agencies that seek to subvert your Church, and undermine your Son's rule, we pray for them to be converted. Like Saul of Tarsus on the road to Damascus, may they be confronted by your Son and his majesty, and call him "Lord" now. And if they will not, bring their power to nothing and their schemes down to the dust.

Now therefore, O kings, be wise; be warned, O rulers of the earth. Serve the LORD with fear, and rejoice with trembling. Kiss the Son, lest he be angry, and you perish in the way, for his wrath is quickly kindled. Blessed are all who take refuge in him. We pray for those of our family, friends and fellows who have turned away from Christ, or have never known him (...). Oh, that they will *"Kiss the Son lest they perish in the way."* We also pray for our brothers and sisters languishing in mental darkness of one kind or another (...); those who are limping along with sickness, disease, or brokenness (...); and those struggling with finances and family issues (...); be their refuge and strength, lifting up their heads and hearts in hope, for truly *"blessed are all those who take refuge in him."* Amen.

19

PSALM 128

Blessed is everyone who fears the LORD, who walks in his ways!
You shall eat the fruit of the labor of your hands; you shall be
blessed, and it shall be well with you. Since Christ loved the
Church and gave himself up for her, that he might sanctify
her, having cleansed her by the washing of water with the
word, we pray for the Church here and world over, for this
congregation, as well as (...). We ask that by blessing of
your Son, by the reforming and revitalizing work of your
Spirit, by the faithful reading, preaching and teaching of
your Scriptures, and by the right administration of your
sacraments, Jesus might present the Church to himself in
splendor, without spot or wrinkle or any such thing, that
she might be holy and without blemish (Ephesians 5:25–
27). Further, we ask you to be with those in our families
and in our congregation, who need heart or healing or help
(...).

Your wife will be like a fruitful vine within your house; your
children will be like olive shoots around your table. Behold, thus
shall the man be blessed who fears the LORD. We remember the
mothers in our lives today, the hours of often selfless toil,
maternal worry, and tender care. We are especially thankful
for the godly mothers who displayed humble, resilient and

affectionate faith! We ask you to draw our mothers closer to you where there is fullness of joy. Give them hope; strengthen, encourage and refresh them. Some here may have sad memories with regard to their mothers; please mend that sadness. Some mothers and their children may be at serious odds with each other; please affect repentance where either mother or child has sinned; and where at all possible, bring reunion and reconciliation.

The LORD bless you from Zion! May you see the prosperity of Jerusalem all the days of your life! May you see your children's children! Peace be upon Israel! Look upon our country, our leaders, the citizens and inhabitants of this land. For the honor of your name; for the sake of your Church; for the advantage of our nation; and for the interest of all who dwell within our borders; may goodness grow, justice thrive, liberty succeed, godliness prosper, education boom, lawfulness rise, civility spread, the economy turn up, and the job market enlarge. And that your people may be a blessing to their host countries, may peace and prosperity prevail through all the nations of this globe.

20

HEIDELBERG CATECHISM 116–129

Our Father Who art in heaven: we come to you trusting and rejoicing that you are our Father through Jesus Christ, and that you will answer us, as promised, with as much readiness as, and more readiness than, our earthly parents. And we trust that we may expect from your almighty power all things necessary for body and soul. Hear us, Father, as we pray.

Hallowed be thy name: Enable us rightly to know, reverence, magnify, and praise you in all your works through which shine forth your power, wisdom, goodness, justice, mercy, and truth; and likewise to so order our whole life, in thought, word, and work, that your name may never be blasphemed but honored and praised on our account.

Thy kingdom come: Preserve and increase your Church, to include this congregation and these churches in our area (...); and so govern us by your Word and Spirit that we may submit ourselves unto you always more and more. Destroy the works of the devil; destroy every power that exalts itself against you; and destroy all wicked devices formed against your holy Word until the full coming of your kingdom where you shall be all in all.

Thy will be done in earth as it is in heaven: Grant that

we and all people—the USA, our state senators, the nations and leaders of the world, may renounce our own will and yield ourselves, without gainsaying, to your will, which alone is good; that so every one may fulfill their task and calling as willingly and truly as the angels do in heaven.

Give us this day our daily bread: Be pleased to provide for all our bodily needs, and for those down with the flu and respiratory illnesses, the ailing and aged, the poor and penniless, and all in need (...) that we may thereby know that you are the only fountain of all good, and so place that trust alone in you.

And forgive us our debts as we forgive our debtors: Be pleased, for the sake of Christ, to forgive our transgressions and evils; and as we find this witness of your grace in us, may our full purpose be to heartily forgive our neighbor. Lord, hear us as we now mention those we need to forgive (...). Forgive them, forgive us, and give us renewed willingness to forgive and pursue reconciliation.

And lead us not into temptation, but deliver us from evil: Since we are so weak in ourselves that we cannot stand even for a moment, while our deadly enemies—the devil, the world, and our own flesh—assail us without ceasing; be pleased to preserve and strengthen us by the power of your Holy Spirit, that we may stand firm against them until we come off at last with complete victory!

All this we ask of you, because as our King who has power over all things, you are both willing and able to give us all good, and thereby we long for your holy name to be glorified now into eternity: *For thine is the kingdom, and the power, and the glory, forever.* **Amen.**

21

PSALM 146

O LORD, you made heaven and earth, the sea and all that is in them; you keep truth forever and execute justice for the oppressed. You give food to the hungry and freedom to the prisoners; you open the eyes of the blind and raise those who are bowed down; you watch over the strangers and relieve the fatherless and widow. It is to you we come!

O LORD, you made heaven and earth, the sea and all that is in them. We pray for your whole Church on earth, including (…). Fill her with all truth, in all truth with all peace. Where she is corrupt, purify her; where she is in error, direct her; where in anything she is amiss, reform her. Where she is right, strengthen her; where she is in need, provide for her; where she is divided, reunite her; for the sake of Jesus Christ your Son our Savior. *The LORD shall reign forever, your God, O Zion, to all generations. Praise the LORD!*[1]

O LORD, you made heaven and earth, the sea and all that is in them. Grant unto us, your children, that by your enlightenment our minds may savor and dwell on what is true and good, and under your merciful protection, may do what is upright, and be filled with joyfulness, peace, and hope. *The*

LORD shall reign forever, your God, O Zion, to all generations. Praise the LORD!

O LORD, you made heaven and earth, the sea and all that is in them. We pray for these (...). We ask you to restore them body and soul in Jesus Christ, give them your relief and comfort, and grant them noteworthy reasons to take heart. *The LORD shall reign forever, your God, O Zion, to all generations. Praise the LORD!*

O LORD, you made heaven and earth, the sea and all that is in them. We remember those in the military, fire department, sheriff's department, and the local police department (...). Give them protection from their enemies, wisdom in the difficult situations, and good leaders. *The LORD shall reign forever, your God, O Zion, to all generations. Praise the LORD!*

O LORD, you made heaven and earth, the sea and all that is in them. Take notice of the nations of the world. Tyranny, violence, slaughter, hunger, machinations, and conspiracies abound. Give peace, O God, give peace in our time that all may dwell securely and successfully in their land and your Church be protected. *The LORD shall reign forever, your God, O Zion, to all generations. Praise the LORD!*

O LORD, you made heaven and earth, the sea and all that is in them. Hear us, O Lord, for our own beloved country. Rid our nation of unbelief and every godless custom; increase the number of those who are not ashamed to confess Christ with integrity of life and talk, who are not afraid to follow his way, that brotherly kindness and civility may abound, and that righteousness would flow from our homes and down our streets like a mighty river. *The LORD shall reign forever, your God, O Zion, to all generations. Praise the LORD!* We ask all this and more in Jesus' name. Amen.

---

1. Adapted from (1979) The Book of Common Prayer, and Administration of the Sacraments, and Other Rites and Ceremonies of the Church, (New York, New York: The Church Hymnary Corporation and Seabury Press), 816.

22

PSALM 111:1-4

Praise the LORD! I will give thanks to the LORD with my whole heart, in the company of the upright, in the congregation. Great are the works of the LORD, studied by all who delight in them. Full of splendor and majesty is his work, and his righteousness endures forever. He has caused his wondrous works to be remembered; the LORD is gracious and merciful. For these reasons we make bold to adore you and to call on you.

For your holy, apostolic Church, with all of her elders, bishops, pastors, deacons, teachers and parishioners, including (…), we pray. May their faith be growing abundantly, and their love for one another increase. May their steadfastness and faith shine brightly, even in the face of persecutions and affliction (2 Thessalonians 1:3–4). We make bold to ask because *the LORD is gracious and merciful.*

For the seminaries in our land, especially Birmingham, Pittsburgh, Beeson, and Dallas Theological Seminaries, we pray. May they foster godliness and piety, shaping and forming good leaders for your Church and missionaries for the harvest. We make bold to ask because *the LORD is gracious and merciful.*

For this congregation; our elders and deacons; our Sunday School teachers; our works of mercy and service through the needlework guild, ESL, and so forth; our generous aid to local projects and ministries; our teaming up with and supporting missionaries; and all you have called us to be and do, we pray. O God of peace, sanctify us completely, making us fully blameless at the coming of our Lord Jesus Christ (1 Thessalonians 5:23). We make bold to ask because *the LORD is gracious and merciful*.

For the nations of the world, teaming with tribes and tongues, we pray. May they seek good, and not evil, that they may live. May they hate evil, and love good, and establish justice in the gate (Amos 5:14–15). We make bold to ask because *the LORD is gracious and merciful*.

For these United States of America, those who govern, and for all the residents and citizens, we pray. May there be justice that rolls down like waters and righteousness like an ever-flowing stream (Amos 5:24). May the tide turn for the better, especially with regard to addictions to opioids, marijuana, gambling, and instant gratification. May our elections result in greater common good. May our dispositions, dialogues and even dissensions be wholesome and heartening. We make bold to ask because *the LORD is gracious and merciful*.

For those in need, the poor, hungry, homeless, unemployed, sick, and lonely; for those whose marriages are rocky or already shattered on the rocks; and those finding that there's more month than money, we pray (…), may they receive the right help at the right time in the right way. And show us how we might be part of the remedy. We make bold to ask because *the LORD is gracious and merciful*.

For those who do not believe in Christ, and those in deep spiritual need, we pray (…), kindle the fire of faith, hope and love in them. We make bold to ask because *the LORD is gracious and merciful*.

We present all of these petitions in Jesus' name because *the LORD is gracious and merciful*. Amen.

23

DEVASTATION AND RENEWAL

O Lord, who knows the thoughts and intentions of our hearts, we pray for the besieged and beleaguered peoples in our world, suffering from floods, droughts, tsunamis, hurricanes, unemployment, military threats, fears and pestilence. Please establish peace, justice, recovery and efficient economies in all lands, for the good of all, so that the Gospel of Jesus may spread unchecked, and that your Church may dwell securely in peace and quietness.

Guide our own leaders in this country to throw off selfish programs, cut-throat tactics, and dastardly devices; and to put on what is truly legitimate and will promote evenhanded integrity.

Give ear to our concerns as we pray for those who are in unbelief and for those who have deserted the Christian faith (...), may they turn around and believe in your Son Jesus Christ, and have everlasting life.

We pray for our enemies that you would lead them and us from prejudice to truth; and deliver them and us from hatred, cruelty and revenge to faith, hope and love; and in your good time enable us all to stand reconciled before you through Jesus Christ your Son.

For your Church in all places, this congregation, and

(…). Our desire is to see all who claim to be your people, to be holy, whole and health-giving in Jesus Christ. Therefore those who have stumbled into errors that dishonor you and create schism, restore them to your way of truth; those who have allowed their desires and ambitions to squeeze out brotherly love and create fights and wars, reinstate them in the cross-shaped ways of Christ; those who are towing the line and promoting decent doctrine and genuine godliness, encourage them by giving grace to the humble as you withstand the proud; and those who are standing firm against the pressures and persecutions of the world, strengthen them that in life and in death they may remain faithful witnesses.

Look upon the many seminaries in our land, those institutions that educate and form leaders for your Church. May these seminaries have the instructors, administrators and money they need to function well. May each campus be an environment of thoughtfulness, decorum and genuine godliness.

Lord, since your eye is on those who fear you, on those who hope in you steadfast love, that you may deliver their soul from death and keep them alive in famine (Psalm 33:18–19), we intercede on behalf of those with cancer, MS, diabetes, Crohn's, dementia, and other ailments (…), lift their hearts, grow them in the Christian virtue of defiant hope—a godly defiance against hopelessness and hollow despair, and do bring them lasting relief.

Thank you for inviting us to pour out our prayers, and promising that as we pray in Jesus' name you hear us and will answer us. Amen.

24

STRONGHOLD FOR THE OPPRESSED

O Lord you are a stronghold for the oppressed, a stronghold in times of trouble. And those who know your name put their trust in you, for you, O Lord, have not forsaken those who seek you (Psalm 9:9–10). It is to you we come to voice our praises and focus our prayers.

That the needy shall not be forgotten and the hope of the poor shall not perish forever, we give you our praise (Psalm 9:18)!

That you have sent us bountiful rains; have provided for us copiously; and have heard our cry for help and sustained us, we give you praise!

That you have watched over our country in the good times and bad; have seen to the affairs of our State; and have looked after the needs and worries of our communities and families, we give you praise!

We implore you to maintain your Church in all places, including this congregation, and (...). Bring unity where there is division; order where there is disorder; faithfulness where there is infidelity; godliness where there is impiety; Gospel where there is legalism; and forgiveness where there are grudges. Hear our Prayer, O Lord!

We implore you for the nations of the world, including

Uganda, Ukraine, United Arab Emirates, and the United Kingdom. Since national entities often think more highly of themselves than they ought, and seek to place themselves above you, and above justice, and above goodness, then we pray with the psalmist: Arise, O Lord! Let not man prevail; let the nations be judged before you! Put them in fear, O Lord! Let the nations know that they are but men (Psalm 9:19–20)! For you are the Lord who sits enthroned forever; you have established your throne for justice, and you judge the world with righteousness; you judge the peoples with uprightness (Psalm 9:7–8). Hear our Prayer, O Lord!

We implore you to oversee our nation, its prosperity and progress, its life and legalities. Preside over our courts, and over the appointments to judicial benches. Bring that which is genuinely good and right to dominate in our land, not Conservatism, or Liberalism, or Progressivism, or Socialism; that which is genuinely good and right for Asian, Black, Latino, White, poor, prosperous, immigrants, residents, urbanite and country folk. Hear our prayer, O Lord!

We implore you to step into the ailments and treatments of those who find their cells and cerebrum failing (…), to take up the recovery of those who are walking in deep darkness or despair (…), to give strength to those who are exhausted and exasperated (…), to aid the insight and direction of those who are deciding on their vocational course (…), to comfort and console those who are grieving over their loved ones (…). Hear our prayer, O Lord!

In Jesus' name we praise you and pray. Amen

25

THE LORD'S PRAYER

Our Father who art in heaven: What an honor to be allowed to call you *Our Father*. As *Father*, you care for us, you invite us, and you look out for us. And as *Our Father* you bring us together with sons and daughters from every ethnic group, economic standing, and educational status. Further, being *Our Father in Heaven*, we rejoice that you are unscathed and unsullied by human sin, shame, scandal, and schemes! Glory to you! **Our Father who art in heaven.**

Hallowed by Thy name: Our chief desire and principal ambition is to glorify you—to hold your honor high; therefore we do pray that your fame and renown, your rightness and righteousness would be accepted and upheld world over—including in Vietnam, Yemen, Zambia, Zimbabwe and our own country. Additionally, our chief desire and principle ambition is to glorify you and enjoy you forever. And so bring us to find our deepest satisfaction in you, our warmest delight in who you are and how you are, no matter our circumstances or situations. **Hallowed be Thy name.**

Thy kingdom come, Thy will be done on earth as it is in heaven: Though your reign has begun coming in the presence and work of your Son, we long for the day when, after you have destroyed every rule, authority and power, placing them all under the feet of your reigning Son, you will destroy that last enemy, death (1 Corinthians 15:24–26)! May all tribes, peoples, clans, kinfolks and nations come to recognize that you have made the crucified and resurrected Jesus both Lord and Messiah, and that we will all stand before his judgment seat to receive what is due for what we have done in the body, whether good or evil (2 Corinthians 5:10). And may this recognition affect and inform all actions, judgments, appointments, taxations, legislations, conflicts and executive decisions now. **Thy kingdom come, Thy will be done on earth as it is in heaven.**

Give us this day our daily bread: Thank you that you have supplied our day-by-day necessities; please continue to do so. We also thank you that you have richly provided us with everything to enjoy. For all your people in all places —including (...), and our own congregation—may we be rich in good works, generous, ready to share. And may we guard the deposit entrusted to us, avoid the irreverent babble and contradictions of what is often called "knowledge" (1 Timothy 6:17–21). **Give us this day our daily bread.**

Forgive us our debts, as we forgive our debtors: We acknowledge that we all too easily hold grudges, savoring the bittersweet satisfactions of our own rightness and how wronged we have been by him or her or them. But thank God, you don't play this manipulative game. May your forgiveness wash over us so thoroughly and freshly that we would let go of the grudges, blame-shifting and sourness, open our hands and hearts, and show as much grace to others as you have shown us. For truly no one has wronged us as much as we have wronged you. **Forgive us our debts, as we forgive our debtors.**

Lead us not into temptation, but deliver us from the

evil one: If anyone is caught in any transgression, may we not excuse it or ignore it, but as instruments in the Redeemer's hand, help us to restore that person in a spirit of gentleness. And help us to keep watch on ourselves, lest we too become tempted. And aid us to bear one another's burdens, and so fulfill the law of Christ (Galatians 6:1–2). Fortify those who are in trouble, overcome with trouble, or just plain troubled (...), may their trials not become a temptation to despair or to break faith with you. And God of peace, come quickly and crush Satan under our feet (Romans 16:20). **Lead us not into temptation, but deliver us from the evil one.**

For Thine is the kingdom, and the power, and the glory, forever. Amen!

26

"NOW THANK WE ALL OUR GOD"

TRINITY HYMNAL 98

God declared to Moses: *"'See now that I, even I, am he, and there is no god beside me; I kill and I make alive; I wound and I heal; and there is none that can deliver out of my hand"* (Deuteronomy 32:39); and Paul proclaimed: *"So then it depends not on human will or exertion, but on God, who has mercy"* (Romans 9:16). "Now thank we all our God, with heart and hands and voices, Who wondrous things has done, in Whom this world rejoices; Who from our mothers' arms has blessed us on our way, with countless gifts of love, and still is ours today."

For those in every nation—including our own country as well as Palau, Palestinian Territories, Panama, and Papua New Guinea—we call upon you to govern their deliberations, machinations, maneuverings, and decisions in such ways as will enhance peace and bring about goodness and rightness.

For your Church in every place, together with this your congregation, and (…), we pray in the words of the hymn: "Oh, may this bounteous God through all our life be near us, With ever joyful hearts and blessed peace to cheer us; And keep us in His grace, and guide us when perplexed; And guard us through all ills in this world, and the next!"

For all who are dispirited and dejected, we pray. Lord, have mercy.

For all who have lost hope, peace and joy, we pray. Lord, have mercy.

For all who are unable to cope or get by, we pray. Lord, have mercy.

For all who are weak, heavy burdened, or spent, we pray. Christ, have mercy.

For all who are in dread, anxious or distressed, we pray. Christ, have mercy.

For all who are dead in their trespasses and sins, have strayed, or are skeptical, we pray. Christ, have mercy.

For all who feel lifeless, lame or benumbed, we pray. Lord, have mercy.

For all who are forsaken, betrayed or slandered, we pray. Lord, have mercy.

For all who are powerless, helpless, or vulnerable, we pray. Lord, have mercy.

"All praise and thanks to God the Father now be given, The Son, and Him Who reigns with Them in highest Heaven—The one eternal God, Whom earth and Heav'n adore; For thus it was, is now, and shall be evermore." Amen.

27

COME, HOLY SPIRIT

Creator God who in the beginning made all things of nothing by the power of your word, and all very good; whose Spirit hovered over all that was formless and void to bring forth order and life. We pray for your Spirit to hover over us; and we pray that your Spirit would continue to cause the earth to bring forth fruit bountifully. We pray: Come, Holy Spirit!

Revealing God, who assigned prophets, judges, and Psalmists—like Moses, Deborah, David and Isaiah—to bring forth your decrees, directions and adulations, and clothed them with your Spirit who guided them and testified through them of the sufferings of Christ and the subsequent glories. Clothe us with your Spirit that we may bravely serve you and our neighbors in love and truth. We pray: Come, Holy Spirit!

Holy God who sent your Son Jesus Christ into the world that through him we might have life; and after his death, burial, resurrection and ascension, you sent forth your Holy Spirit by your Son, so that we would not be left as orphans. May we know that our Lord Jesus is with us and we are with you. And we ask this especially on behalf of those facing surgery, chemotherapy, and physical troubles, loss, and shadowy insecurities (...). We pray: Come, Holy Spirit!

God and Father of our Lord Jesus Christ, who sent the Spirit of Truth to bear witness of Jesus, and by his indwelling presence makes us able to also bear witness of our Lord: pour down your rousing and refreshing goodness on us and your people all over the world—including (...). We pray: Come, Holy Spirit!

Sovereign, saving God whose Son sent the *paracletos*, the helper/counselor, who comes to convict the world concerning sin and righteousness and judgment: concerning sin, because they do not believe in your Son; concerning righteousness, because he has ascended to your right hand, and we presently see him no longer; concerning judgment, because the ruler of this world is judged (John 16:8–11). May the Spirit continue to convict our world— including the USA, New Zealand, Nicaragua, Niger, and Nigeria—concerning sin, righteousness and judgment, that all the world may turn to you and live. We pray: Come, Holy Spirit!

Adopting God, who gave us your Spirit of adoption by whom we can cry out "Abba, Father!" May your Spirit bear witness with our spirits that we are your children, no matter what our society shouts at us; no matter what the devil whispers to us; no matter what our defeats and frustrations gossip to us; no matter what our tired and trembling hearts sigh to us! We pray: Come, Holy Spirit!

Sanctifying God, whose will for us is holiness and so you have given us the Holy Spirit. May righteousness, peace and joy in the Holy Spirit run deep in us and blossom beautifully forth from us; and so fill us with joy and peace in believing that we may abound in hope by the power of the Holy Spirit. We pray: Come, Holy Spirit!

In Christ's name we pray: Come, Holy Spirit! Amen.

28

1 KINGS 8:45

Almighty God, Heavenly Father, you have summoned us to pray for the Church and the world, that your grace and salvation might become known to all. And you have promised that as we pray in the name of your Son Jesus Christ, you hear us and answer us. And so we pray in the name of Christ, *hear in heaven our prayer and our plea, and maintain our cause* (1 Kings 8:45).

For those in need (...); the poor and the hungry (...); the homeless and unemployed (...); those hit by the wildfires and those helping to rebuild (...); the sick and lonely (...); may they receive the right help at the right time in their distress, and find real relief. And so we pray, *hear in heaven our prayer and our plea, and maintain our cause* (1 Kings 8:45).

For those who have not yet believed (...); all in spiritual need (...); and those who have stumbled and fallen (...); bring them faith, hope and comfort in Jesus Christ. And so we pray, *hear in heaven our prayer and our plea, and maintain our cause* (1 Kings 8:45).

For the peace and security of the nations of this world—including Mali, Malta, Marshall Islands, and Mauritania; for the end of war and violent oppression; and for the end of exploitation and eradication; that there may be peace in our times so that the peoples of the earth may receive the Prince of Peace. And so we pray, *hear in heaven our prayer and our plea, and maintain our cause* (1 Kings 8:45).

For our own country, those who govern and misgovern, and for all the people—free born, foreign born and unborn —that we may have justice, security, and well-being. And continue the appropriate rains and showers we need for our crops, cattle, privations and provisions. And so we pray, *hear in heaven our prayer and our plea, and maintain our cause* (1 Kings 8:45).

For your one, holy, catholic and apostolic Church— including (...)—for her pastors and leaders and all her people; that they may be faithful to the Word of God and prove to be the light of Christ to the nations of the world. And so we pray, *hear in heaven our prayer and our plea, and maintain our cause* (1 Kings 8:45).

For our own congregation, our elders and deacons, those who give their time and toil to teach Sunday School, those who serve quietly and unobserved, the parents with children in the home, and each of us in our vocations; may we prove to be Christ's disciples in both word and deed. And so we pray, *hear in heaven our prayer and our plea, and maintain our cause* (1 Kings 8:45).

For the children we are supporting and caring for through Compassion International, and their families: (...). May our monies, prayers and letters truly help them. May they flourish in health and education and have clean drinking water. And may they know you and your Son Jesus Christ. And so, we pray in the name of Christ, *hear in heaven our prayer and our plea, and maintain our cause* (1 Kings 8.45). Amen.

29

PSALM 147:11

Our Father, whose blessed Son our Savior gave his back to the smiters and did not hide his face from shame: give us all that we need to endure the sufferings of this present time with grace and joy, as well as a sure and certain confidence of the glory that shall be revealed in us through Jesus Christ our Lord. *For the LORD takes pleasure in those who fear him, in those who hope in his steadfast love* (Psalm 147:11).

O Lord, we pray for your Church in all places, for this congregation, and (...). Help us that we may be strengthened to greater and greater faithfulness, that no matter what we may face, we will always walk in your ways. Take care of all our needs, providing for us bountifully from your generosity. *For the LORD takes pleasure in those who fear him, in those who hope in his steadfast love.*

Please turn the hearts of our enemies away from hate and maliciousness and bring them into your fold. And give us daily grace to love our enemies, do good, and lend, hoping for nothing in return, that we may show ourselves to be sons of the Most High. *For the LORD takes pleasure in those who fear him, in those who hope in his steadfast love.*

We beseech you to lift up your face on those in hard times, dark times, dry times, and harrowing times (...).

Comfort them in their grief; strengthen them in their weakness; deliver them in their distress; refresh them in their weariness and raise them to renewed hope and with refreshed hearts. *For the LORD takes pleasure in those who fear him, in those who hope in his steadfast love.*

Please safeguard our country and deliver us from the road to serfdom. Be with our State leaders and teachers, and bring forth a proper, appropriate and prompt solution. Direct the hearts and minds of the leaders of every nation, including Lithuania, Luxembourg, Macau and Macedonia, that they would render true judgments, show kindness and mercy to one another, they would not oppress the widow, the fatherless, the sojourner, or the poor, nor devise evil against another in their heart (Zechariah 7:9–10). *For the LORD takes pleasure in those who fear him, in those who hope in his steadfast love.*

Father, we pray for those we know or have met who are in real need, and we pray for those who play on the vulnerabilities and emotions of others; for people who mishandle their resources and people who perform for drugs and drink; for people who are genuinely poor and those who are being devious and deceitful, (...). Help us to fathom and perceive who it is that genuinely needs aid, and how best and rightly to help them. And also, grant to them a new way, your new way, that they may be freed from lifestyles and life-long habits that are destructive and demeaning. *For the LORD takes pleasure in those who fear him, in those who hope in his steadfast love.*

Finally, Lord, we thank you for your generous goodness to us, and that you take pleasure in those who fear you, in those who hope in your steadfast love. Amen.

30

SHALOM

Unlike Marduk and the gods of the nations, when you made humankind, you said: *"Behold, **I have given you** every plant yielding seed that is on the face of all the earth, and every tree with seed in its fruit. You shall have them for food. And to every beast of the earth and to every bird of the heavens and to everything that creeps on the earth, everything that has the breath of life, **I have given** every green plant for food." And it was so"* (Genesis 1:29–30). Truly, Lord God, you made us not because you needed us. You made us not because you were lonely and lacked love. You made us not because you needed us to scratch some itch. You made us because you are love and goodness, and so desired to give and lavish that love and goodness on us! Therefore, with the twenty-four elders and creatures that surround your throne, we adore and worship you: *"Worthy are you, our Lord and God, to receive glory and honor and power, for you created all things, and by your will they existed and were created"* (Revelation 4:11). Hear us now, O Lord, as we pray:

For the peace and security of all the nations of this world, including Iceland, India, Indonesia, and Iran, we pray to you Lord. O God, hear our prayer; give ear to the words of our mouth (Psalm 54:2).

For the safety and godly direction of the president of these United States, our legislators, and judiciary, we pray to you Lord. O God, hear our prayer; give ear to the words of our mouth.

For the wellbeing and achievement of our state, counties, cities, and townships, we pray to you Lord. O God, hear our prayer; give ear to the words of our mouth.

For fitting and seasonable weather and rain, the abundance of the fruits of the earth, and the speedy end of the flu season, we pray to you Lord. O God, hear our prayer; give ear to the words of our mouth.

For the strength and recovery of the older ones, infirm, sick, and suffering ones, we pray to you Lord (...). O God, hear our prayer; give ear to the words of our mouth.

For the deliverance of the poor, oppressed, unemployed, destitute, prisoners, and captives, we pray to you Lord. O God, hear our prayer; give ear to the words of our mouth.

For the *shalom* and goodness of God to flood our lives and keep us steady and sturdy when we are anxious and fearful, we pray to you Lord. O God, hear our prayer; give ear to the words of our mouth.

For the salvation of those who are still dead in their trespasses and sins, and for the rescue of those who have forgotten their savior, we pray to you Lord (...). O God, hear our prayer; give ear to the words of our mouth.

For the Church throughout the earth, this congregation, as well as (...); that we may grow in the grace and knowledge of Jesus Christ our Lord, we pray to you Lord. O God, hear our prayer; give ear to the words of our mouth.

All we ask in union with Jesus Christ your Son, and our Lord and Savior. O God, hear our prayer; give ear to the words of our mouth. Amen.

31

CHRIST IS RISEN

Our Father, who has told us to cast our burden on you and promised that you will sustain us, and that you shall never permit the righteous to be shaken (Psalm 55:22); we confidently lift up to you our petitions and supplications, because *Christ is risen; he is risen indeed!*

We remember those who find themselves fraught with specific hardships, fears, worries and perplexities, and others who have been fractured by these adversities (...); raise them up in new-found hope; comforting, healing, restoring, and defending them where most needed; since *Christ is risen; he is risen indeed!*

Guide the nations of the earth, the USA, Liberia, Libya, and Liechtenstein, in the practices that foster peace and tranquility, and in proper ways so that all may prosper, and your people may be safe. We pray for our region that you would be pleased to grant us to thrive economically, educationally, artistically and ethically. All this we ask because *Christ is risen; he is risen indeed!*

Further, we pray that you would be with those in our neighborhoods where we live, on these streets and housing divisions (...). Please turn our suburbs and subdivisions into real neighborhoods and communities of caring people who treat one another with respect, interest, kindness and friendliness and will look out for each other's best interests. And may it be known in our neighborhoods that *Christ is risen; he is risen indeed!*

O Lord, we pray for your Church in all places, for this congregation, and (...). Strengthen what is true, good, wholesome and right among us, and guide us away from what is harmful and false; *for Christ is risen; he is risen indeed!*

We implore you to change the hearts and dispositions of our enemies that kindness and civility might reign; and grant them new hearts to love you and be drawn into your family through Christ; to show to all that *Christ is risen; he is risen indeed!*

We plead for your sovereign grace to grip the hearts and minds of many, to bring some to salvation and to bring others to restoration (...), so that all may come to know and rejoice in the fact that *Christ is risen; he is risen indeed!*

Finally, Lord, we thank you for your generous goodness to us (...). And we offer our thanks joyfully as we say together: *Christ is risen; he is risen indeed!* Amen.

III

YOUR FACE, O LORD, DO I SEEK

This final chapter is about specific prayers. Clearly it is not exhaustive, but it may hold just the petition needed in tight and difficult situations. Once more, these stand-alone requests are shaped and formed by Scripture.

1

CHILDREN, IN UTERO AND MISCARRIED

Lord God, to whom even the darkness is not dark; the night is bright as the day, for darkness is as light with you. Who formed our inward parts; knitted us together in our mother's womb. We praise you, for we are fearfully and wonderfully made. Wonderful are your works; our soul knows it very well (Psalm 139:12–14). We remember those of our children and grandchildren who are still being formed by your skillful hands in their mother's wombs. Smile on their gestation and may they each come forth always trusting in you and your goodness. But we also remember before you those who never saw the light of day, as well as those who quickly passed away (…). Thank you for the little moment their mamas and daddies had with them. Thank you for the brief kick or movement in their mother's womb. We believe your Son when he said the kingdom of heaven is heavily populated with *brephas*, with pre-born and newborn children. Give soothing stillness and healthful wholeness to their mothers and fathers. O Lord, hear our prayer.

2

HEARTBROKEN

We pray for those, who like Job, find themselves with broken hearts, crying out "Why?!" and surrounded by those who will not or cannot understand. We pray for those who find their hearts broken because loved ones have betrayed them or violated their trust. We pray for those whose hearts are broken because of grief and loss (...). Lord, who heals the brokenhearted and binds up their wounds (Psalm 147:3), break through their dark clouds with the light of your face lifted up on them. Bring your favor to rest upon them, and aid them toward wholeness, and to rejoice in you and all of your goodness. O Lord, hear our prayer.

3

MESSED-UP LINEAGE

Sometimes we recount that you are the Lord who is merciful and gracious, slow to anger and abounding in steadfast love (Psalm 103.8), and it barely registers on our hearts. But here we declare it and give you thanks for it! You are the God of Noah who once got drunk and was shamed by his son. The God of Abraham who lied about Sarah, and who tried to give you a hand through Hagar, messing up so much. The God of Judah, who was self-serving; and Tamar, who once was cunningly incestuous. You are the God of Rahab who refused to be held back by her sexual trysts and ethnic lineage and courageously owned you as her God against all odds. You are the God of Ruth who was a homeless immigrant. You are the God of David, a man after your own heart who broke your heart in his murderous power play, but you still loved him and turned him around. The God of Bathsheba who betrayed her filial loyalty, and yet you made her an honorable woman. The God who gladly brought your Son into the world, born of this bloodline, to save his people from their sins! Truly you are the Lord who is merciful and gracious, slow to anger and abounding in steadfast love. Shower your gracious mercy on us; and turn around those who think they are too far gone (...). O Lord, hear our prayer.

4

FOR THE OPPRESSED

O Lord, a stronghold for the oppressed, a stronghold in times of trouble. Those who know your name put their trust in you, for you, O Lord, have not forsaken those who seek you (Psalm 9:9–10). We pray for you to hear the cries of those children oppressed by adults; those husbands and wives browbeaten by their spouses; those men, women, girls and boys exploited by the powerful (...). As you rescued your people from the heavy hand of Pharaoh, hear their cries and bring them release and relief. And for the tormentors and toughs who try to physically, emotionally, or verbally beat others into submission, we pray (...). Bring them to their knees in repentance. And if they will not repent, then: *"Arise, O LORD; O God, lift up your hand; forget not the afflicted...Break the arm of the wicked and evildoer; call his wickedness to account till you find none"* (Psalm 10:12, 15). O Lord, hear our prayer.

5

THE ENTRAPPED

Lord, mighty and strong, a refuge in the storm and a shelter in the squall—you see clearly through the fog of human confusion, the stifling smoke of worry, the crushing blanket of darkness of depression—you set captives free, open prison doors and release the entrapped, lift up the oppressed and put the oppressors down. O Lord, mighty and strong, liberating and loving: hear us as we pray for these (...). You see clearly what is going on, you hear the groans, know the tears, understand the fears and worries, are wise to the traps. Move in their lives and over their circumstances and set them free—free from their own sins and the sins of others; free from the hurt and pain; free from their own narrow confinements. Set them up in a broad place in full daylight and the fresh air. Strengthen the weak hands and feeble knees; make them run and not grow weary, to walk and not faint. Raise them up on eagles' wings (Is. 40:31. O Lord, hear our prayer.

6

TROUBLED IN HOME AND HEART

Turn your eyes and care onto those who are having trouble and turmoil in their marriages or with their children (...); those who find that life hasn't gone where they had dreamed and are disheartened (...); and those who are in the ravenous grip of rapacious urges (...). Because you have not given us a spirit of fear, but the Spirit of power, love and self-control (2 Timothy 1:7), fortify them with the righteous resilience to work through their situation, looking above, where Christ is, seated at your right hand, and to turn neither to the right hand or to the left. O Lord, hear our prayer.

7

ROCKY MARRIAGES

God, you know the thoughts and intentions of our hearts, our dreams, our schemes, and our plans, and you know the depth and darkness of our hurts. You are the one who can change the hearts of men and women, steering their direction; and so we implore you on behalf of those whose marriages are on the rocks (...), that you would comfort them in their angst, anguish and anger. Where one partner is stubbornly resisting and stonewalling the other partner, we ask you to bring about changes in perspective, softening of heart, and a renewed commitment to their marriage. Where both parties need to seek forgiveness from each other, show them and give them the courage to do so. And where they need to extend forgiveness to each other, direct them. We ask all of this with longing and yearning hearts. O Lord, hear our prayer.

8

ANXIETY

Lord God of Sabaoth, you have recorded for us these words of deep comfort: *"Strengthen the weak hands, and make firm the feeble knees. Say to those who have an anxious heart, "Be strong; fear not! Behold, your God will come with vengeance, with the recompense of God. He will come and save you"* (Isaiah 35:3–4). We pray for the anxious and the forlorn, especially those we know (…). Break through the dark walls that have been set up around their assessments; pull back the thick curtains they have around the eyes of their hearts; and bring the light of your face to shine on their lives that their weak hands may be strengthened and their feeble knees made firm. O Lord, hear our prayer.

9

THOSE IN PRISON

You who are Father of the fatherless and protector of widows, who settles the solitary in a home; leads out the prisoners to prosperity, but brings the rebellious to dwell in a parched land (Psalm 68:5–6): we pray for those now in prison. So many, though not all, have come from broken homes, fatherless homes, and violent homes. It is no excuse for their criminal activities, but it causes us great concern. We pray that you will visit them with your mercy and grace that they may come to truly know you as Father of the fatherless and help of the homeless. Bring them to genuine repentance and away from jailhouse religion. We pray this especially for those presently on death row. Bless and enhance those who visit prisoners to show them better ways and The Better Way of Jesus. For those who have been jailed unjustly, we pray that their innocence will become clear as day, and they would be released and restored. O Lord, hear our prayer.

10

CRIME VICTIMS AND THEIR FAMILIES

Just as you were conscious of your peoples' affliction in Egypt as they suffered at the cruel hands of their task masters and said "I have surely seen the affliction of my people who are in Egypt and have heard their cry because of their taskmasters. I know their sufferings" (Exodus 3:7); so you have heard the cries and weeping of those who have suffered from wrongdoing, and those whose loved ones have fallen at the hands of criminals (...). We pray for the living victims that evil may be crushed, and their lives and wellbeing restored. We pray for the families grieving the violent death of those they loved that you would comfort them in their heartache, bring justice to bear, and give them hope, even in the hurt. O Lord, hear our prayer.

11

ADDICTIONS

Lord Jesus, who at your ascension ascended on high, led a host of captives in your train and received gifts among men, even among the rebellious, (Psalm 68:18): we pray for those who are shackled and trapped in their addictions (...). Your resurrection and ascension emancipates the enslaved and restores liberty to the caged. May they come to know you and find you redeeming and releasing them, and see you set their lives in order and equip them to aid others into liberation. O Lord, hear our prayer.

12

MEDIA

Almighty God, the lips of the wise spread knowledge; not so the hearts of fools (Proverbs 15:7). We acknowledge that truth can come through many voices; and falsehood can appear very plausible. Therefore, we implore you to direct, in our time, those who speak where many listen and write what many read in our country. May they do their part in making our hearts wise, our minds sound, our perceptions clear, and our resolve righteous. O Lord, hear our prayer.

13

SEXUAL SINS

Almighty God, mighty in compassion and mighty in kindness, be with those who are struggling with sexual sins (…). May they battle them, and may you be pleased to give them liberty over the sins they are battling with. In Augustine's words: command what you will and give what you command! Set them free from the evil affections and fill them with longing for you and the satisfaction of knowing you. Place them among other believers who will be able to walk with them, care for them, and encourage them in the ways of sanctification. O Lord, hear our prayer.

14

THOSE WITH DISABILITIES

Lord, we ask you to make your love and compassion known to our neighbors with disabilities and infirmities (...). We ask that you would bring them to see themselves as you see them: made in your image. We pray that they would have fruitful and deep relationships and friendships that would not only encourage them personally but would also point them to you and your truth. As a church we ask you to help us to be hospitable to every person who comes through our doors. As neighbors, please equip us with the knowledge and skills to properly support our neighbors who are disabled. And thank you for the agencies and ministries who give support and aid to those with disabilities. May they continue to have the funds and the workers they need, and may they not get burned out. O Lord, hear our prayer.

15

THOSE DELUDED

O Lord, who keeps faith forever; who executes justice for the oppressed; who gives food to the hungry; who sets the prisoners free; who opens the eyes of the blind; who lifts up those who are bowed down; who loves the righteous; who watches over the sojourners; who upholds the widow and the fatherless; but the way of the wicked you bring to ruin (Psalm 146:6–9): we pray for those who are deluded or self-deluded, and in their delusion are ravaging their families, breaking faith with their friends, vandalizing trust and love (…). Open their blind eyes to see themselves for who they are and what they are doing that they may no longer fault others for their own failures, turn, confess their sins, and find you forgiving them and cleansing them of all unrighteousness. O Lord, hear our prayer.

16

HOW TO AID

Mighty God, we often pray for you to do amazing things in peoples' lives, and we know that is right and good, because you are the giver of all good things, you are the restorer of fortunes and fitness. Yet we also know that you have called us to often be instruments in your redeeming, rescuing hands. Help us to see clearly how we should engage the gifts and abilities you have enriched us with to aid others. We need thoughtful wisdom, we need discernment, and we need sensitivity. O God, help us, use us, lead us! O Lord, hear our prayer.

SCRIPTURE INDEX

ABOUT THE AUTHOR

Michael W. Philliber is a twenty-year active duty Air Force veteran (1979–1999). Two years after he retired from the U.S. Air Force, he graduated from Reformed Theological Seminary-Jackson, Mississippi, and was ordained in 2001 in the Presbyterian Church in America. He has been Senior Pastor of Heritage Presbyterian Church (PCA) in Oklahoma City, Oklahoma since 2016. Philliber has also been a Hospice chaplain, and the director of chaplains at the Midland Police Department, Midland, Texas, from 2004 to 2012. He is the author of *Gnostic Trends in the Local Church* and a prolific book reviewer. He has posted over 350 book reviews on his blog, mphilliber.blogspot.com.

ABOUT WHITE BLACKBIRD BOOKS

White blackbirds are extremely rare, but they are real. They are blackbirds that have turned white over the years as their feathers have come in and out over and over again. They are a redemptive picture of something you would never expect to see but that has slowly come into existence over time.

There is plenty of hurt and brokenness in the world. There is the hopelessness that comes in the midst of lost jobs, lost health, lost homes, lost marriages, lost children, lost parents, lost dreams, loss.

But there also are many white blackbirds. There are healed marriages, children who come home, friends who are reconciled. There are hurts healed, children fostered and adopted, communities restored. Some would call these events entirely natural, but really they are unexpected miracles.

The books in this series are not commentaries, nor are they meant to be the final word. Rather, they are a collage of biblical truth applied to current times and places. The authors share their poverty and trust the Lord to use their words to strengthen and encourage his people. Consider these books as entries into the discussion.

May this series help you in your quest to know Christ as he is found in the Gospel through the Scriptures. May you look for and even expect the rare white blackbirds of God's redemption through Christ in your midst. May you be thankful when you look down and see your feathers have turned. May you also rejoice when you see that others have been unexpectedly transformed by Jesus.

Made in the USA
Coppell, TX
18 September 2020

38227656R00090